MW00447117

MICROSOFT 2016 2013 POWERPOINT 2010 2007

TIPS, *Tricks* AND SHORTCUTS

PLUS LINKS TO TRAINING VIDEOS!

PRESENTATIONS, SPECIAL EFFECTS AND ANIMATIONS IN 25 MINI-LESSONS

FULL COLOR VERSION

by

Amelia Griggs

Importing Excel Information + Files

* make into a chart → highlight →
   Insert + recommended chart

* can link data so when you change in one
   (excel vs PPT) it changes data in the other
   = Paste Special →
      Microsoft Excel worksheet object

* Copy chart data - can also link data.
   If it doesn't work -
      File - Info - Edit links to files
         can also break links

* create presentation around photos
   Insert - photo album - can insert all / some
   from file destination.

* copy/paste will paste object in exact location of
   previous slide

Table of Contents

word doc → PPT

in word → outlining → Level 1 (Header)
                      Level 2 (Body)

About This Book

HOW TO USE THIS BOOK

This book is designed for you: the busy, modern learner who needs quick and easy-to-follow instructions at your fingertips. The intention of this book and its contents is to help you master Microsoft PowerPoint features through short mini-lessons. If you are already using Microsoft PowerPoint, you can use this book as a quick reference guide to learn more efficient ways to create awesome presentations, animations, and special effects. If you are brand new to PowerPoint, this book will help you learn how to use this powerful software program with ease at your own pace. Feel free to browse through the Table of Contents to select specific topics that you want to learn right away. Since this book is packed with lots of tips, tricks, and even some secrets, you can pick and choose the features that are right for you.

WHAT'S INCLUDED IN THIS BOOK

This book contains a collection of tips, tricks, and shortcuts presented within 25 mini-lessons. Each lesson contains step-by-step instructions for you to follow. In addition, each section contains a link to a companion video, so you can see the steps in action as well.

It's not always easy to learn all the ins and outs of what a software program has to offer. PowerPoint is no exception. For many of us, there's usually limited time throughout the day to learn all the time-saving shortcuts, let alone discover all the extra bells and whistles. Many times, after we learn the bare minimum features needed to complete our tasks, we stop there and put off the rest until later. And later turns into weeks, months, or sometimes, never. Whether you've been using Microsoft PowerPoint for years, or just recently started using it, this book will help you learn how to use PowerPoint more efficiently and effectively – thereby allowing you to create more dazzling presentations in a snap!

Our busy schedules leave us little time and energy to sit through hours and hours of software training, only to discover that by the end of the day, we can only remember a small portion of what we learned. Instead of watching a two-hour video, or reading a 200-page instruction manual, what if we can easily pick and choose only what we need? What we really need are short, easy-to-follow lessons to help us absorb the information quickly and retain it in our own brains for much longer. That's why I designed this book with the modern learner in mind.

"Creativity is intelligence having fun."

~ Albert Einstein

BITE-SIZED LEARNING

Micro-learning or "bite-sized learning" allows us to learn small bits of knowledge quickly. It's just like eating small meals, which are easier to digest, vs. eating a 7-course meal, which makes you feel stuffed and bloated. It's the same with learning. If you take too much in at once, you run the risk of experiencing cognitive overload.

The short, to-the-point lessons in this book allow you to absorb small amounts of meaningful information in a brief amount of time. Also, you can pick and choose to learn what's best for you.

WHAT VERSIONS OF POWERPOINT DOES THIS BOOK APPLY TO?

All instructions and shortcuts in this book have been tested in Microsoft PowerPoint 2016, 2013, 2010 and 2007. Microsoft PowerPoint 2016 is shown in most of the screen prints in this book. However, if there are any major differences between versions, it is noted throughout the book.

I hope you find the content in this book very helpful!

BONUS! Companion Videos

For each of the 25 sections in this book, there is a companion training video. You can search for each video using the corresponding hashtag. Here's how:

1. Navigate to www.youtube.com
2. In the search box, enter the hashtag search word provided at the end of each section (remember to include "#") which is *#ezppt+[the video number]*. For example:
   > To locate video #1, search for: *#ezppt1*
   > To locate video #2, search for: *#ezppt2*
   > ...and so forth...
   > To locate video #20, search for: *#ezppt20*
3. Click Search (the magnifying glass icon).

Each video contains demonstrations of all the instructions included in each section in this book, plus some additional information. Be sure to check out each training video to see the steps in action and learn even more!

To see all available training videos, visit the the Easy Learning YouTube channel at: www.youtube.com/user/easylearningweb or scan the image below:

From the Easy Learning channel, click "PLAYLISTS" to see training videos grouped by topic. See the PLAYLIST entitled "Microsoft PowerPoint How-To Videos" to see all Microsoft PowerPoint training videos.

Part I: *PowerPoint Basics*

Contents

PowerPoint Basics

What is PowerPoint and What Can It Be Used For?

Creating a Simple Presentation

Simple and Advanced Formatting

Copy/Paste Tricks and the Format Painter

Opening, Saving, Closing, and Printing Presentations

#1: What is PowerPoint and What Can It Be Used For?

Microsoft PowerPoint is a presentation graphics software program that allows you to create and show a series of slides containing text, graphics, and multimedia. Microsoft PowerPoint is one member of the Microsoft Office suite which you can utilize in the Microsoft Windows environment. There are also versions for MAC O/S, Android, and iOS devices.

First, let's review the components of the PowerPoint screen. The familiar **Menu Bar** (**File**, **Home**, **Insert**, etc.) is shown at the top of the image below. Beneath the **Menu Bar** is the **Ribbon**. The **Ribbon** will change depending on what option is selected in the **Menu Bar**.

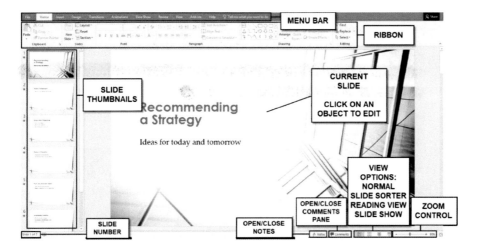

What can PowerPoint be used for?

Microsoft PowerPoint can be used to create:

- Simple or complex slides to accompany a presentation with a slide show
- A self-running slideshow containing images, music, and other multimedia
- An interactive PDF document with links to other pages within the PDF or with links to external websites
- A video to showcase graphics, photos, and other multimedia
- Step-by-step training on any topic
- A quick reference guide or infographic

PowerPoint offers a variety of templates and themes to choose from. To view PowerPoint templates, click **File** -> **New**.

To help you narrow down templates for a specific topic or category, you can:

- Enter one or more search terms in the search box and click the magnifying glass to search for templates related to a topic or phrase. For example, type "training" to see all templates related to training presentations; or type "business plan" to see only business plan themed templates.
- Click on a specific template category including **Presentations**, **Business**, **Education**, **Industry**, **Personal**, **Charts**, and **Diagrams**, to see only templates in that category. Note: In PowerPoint 2007, categories are in the left pane, and only the Blank Presentation shows initially.
- Click on the **Blank Presentation** (white thumbnail) to start from scratch with a blank slide.
- Single click on a template (other than **Blank Presentation**) to zoom in and see an enlarged view of the template.
- Download a template by double-clicking on the thumbnail image, or by clicking **Create** (in PowerPoint 2007, click **Download**).

Some templates are blank with placeholder text boxes for you to fill in, while others have sample content and graphics. The possibilities are endless, so give it a try!

Note: Templates may vary in different versions of Microsoft PowerPoint.

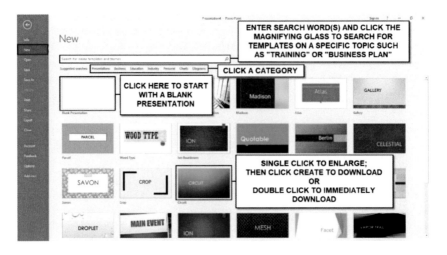

Design ideas - pop up on right when choosing template

In newer versions of PowerPoint, the available templates as well as the thumbnail preview is much improved, allowing you to see more than one slide, color themes, and a more detailed description.

In PowerPoint 2013 and 2016, from the list of template thumbnails, if you single-click on a thumbnail image, you can:

- Click on the left or right arrows to go to the **Previous** or **Next** template in an enlarged view.
- Select a different color scheme for the template.
- Click **Create** to download the template (click **Download** in older versions of PowerPoint).

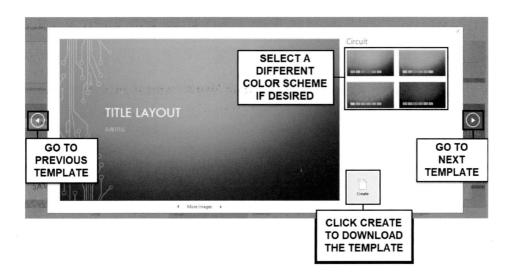

View Companion Video #1 to see these steps in action

Go to www.youtube.com and search for *#ezppt1*

Quickstarter - helps guide you through steps to build presentation.

13

File → Options

* Save — embed fonts = typeface stored
* Proofing — can add grammar
* Advanced — Display = # of presentation (50→20)
* Slide show — end w/ black screen

* <u>Customize Ribbon</u> *
    - Can add a custom tab → Favorites
      select location — new tab
      Can choose commands <u>NOT</u> in Ribbon
      commands you use <u>regularly</u>

- can import & export all customizations (quick access
  toolbar / Ribbon) = when you get new
  computer.

    * Add-ins — people may have purchased
      powerpoint addins (ibEXX)

- File → Protect presentation → encrypt w/ password
  (when saving on public /shared folders)

- Inspect presentation — to clean up behind the scenes
    * Inspect document — off-slide content, comments
  ↳ clean up feature

- Can create custom color themes
            Fonts — option on bottom

    * can save all these
    customizations as a "theme" = custom theme.

*Can use different themes within a template.

#2: *Creating a Simple Presentation Using a Template*

Scenario # 1: You are a new member of a sales team, and you are facilitating a sales strategy meeting in one week. You have an outline and the content for what you need to cover. You have been asked to create a presentation using PowerPoint. You haven't used PowerPoint much, but you've heard there are some ready-to-use templates that may help. Where do you begin?

1. Click **File**-> **New**.
2. In the search box, type **meeting** and click the magnifying glass to search (or press Enter).
3. Several matches are found. Results may vary in different versions of PowerPoint.

4. Single click on the first thumbnail to preview the template.
5. In the template preview (beginning in PowerPoint 2013), do the following to learn more about the template slides (if using PowerPoint 2007 or 2010, download the template to view more):
    a. Click the **More Images** arrows at the bottom center to browse through the template slides. This template contains placeholder text which makes it easy to enter content.
    b. Click the right arrow in the circle on the right to preview the next template. Repeat as needed. Click the left arrow to return to previous templates.
    c. Click **Create** to download the template to begin editing content and creating your presentation. In the example below, the first template was downloaded.

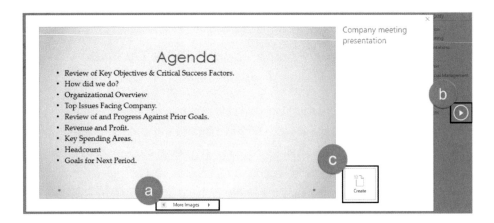

6. Once the template is downloaded, all slides display as thumbnails on the left, and slide 1 displays in the main pane on the right. To see how the template looks as a slide show, click **Slide Show**-> **From Beginning**. While viewing the slide show, click anywhere to continue to the next slide, or press **PageDown (PgDn)** or **PageUp (PgUp)** keys on your keyboard to navigate. Press the **Escape** key (**Esc**) anytime to return to **Normal** view. When you are back to **Normal** view, here are some tips to get started:

   - To navigate to different slides, press the down arrow on your keyboard to move downward or the up arrow to move upward. Alternatively, you can use your mouse to click on a thumbnail on the left to jump to any slide.
   - Click inside a text box on a slide to customize the text (the frame changes to a dotted line and a blinking cursor displays within the text box). **Quick Tip:** To replace all text in a text box, press **CTRL + A** to select all text and then immediately begin typing new text. To select and replace one line (one paragraph) of text, triple click and then begin typing new text.
   - To delete a text box or other object, single click on the edge to select it (the frame changes to a solid line when selected); then press **Delete** on your keyboard.
   - To delete an entire slide, click on the slide thumbnail on the left, and then press **Delete** on your keyboard. You can also right-click on the slide thumbnail and press **Delete**.

7. To learn more about editing and formatting, see section #3 in this book. Remember to save your new file frequently via **File-> Save**. To learn more about saving presentations, see section #5.

Scenario # 2: You are a student, and you have a homework assignment to showcase a collection of pictures. You get extra points if there is some animation in your presentation. Your assignment is due tomorrow, so you need to create a presentation in a hurry! Where do you begin?

1. Click **File-> New**.
2. Try different searches to filter the templates.
   - In this example, enter the words **photos animation** in the search box and press Enter. Several matches are found. Results may vary in different versions of PowerPoint. You can also search using just the word **pictures**, or just the word **photos** which may yield more results to choose from.
3. Review the template descriptions under each template. In newer versions of PowerPoint, hover over an image to see the full description.
4. In this example, a template entitled **Animation slide: Multiple images in a slide show (widescreen)** is selected. Note: This particular template is available in PowerPoint 2013 and 2016. Click to select the template; then click **Create**.
5. Once the template is downloaded, you notice there is one slide showing, so you're not sure what the slide show will look like or how to customize it. First, click **Slide Show-> From Beginning** to preview the slide show.
6. The preview shows how several images are shown with a fade effect. You like it and it's perfect for what you need. You notice there are instructions in the right pane. To replace the images with your other own, do the following:
   a. Click **Home-> Select-> Selection Pane**.
   b. Click the eye icon to hide or show an object.
   c. To quickly and easily change a sample image:
      - Using the **Selection Pane**, click on the image description you want to replace (Picture 2, Picture 10, etc.). Remember to use the eye icon to hide/show to help you identify objects which may be overlapping.

- Next, click the **Format** tab in the **Ribbon** to view format options (you can also double-click on the image on your slide which will open the **Format** tab).
- Click **Change Picture** in the Ribbon.
- Select **From File** (or **From Online Resources**) and select your new image.

7. If you have a lot of images, you may need to duplicate the slides so you can incorporate more images into the template. To duplicate a slide, just right click on the thumbnail on the left and click **Duplicate** slide. Repeat step 6 above to replace the images as needed.

Voila! Your slide show showcasing your images with animation is completed! Remember to save your new file frequently via **File-> Save**. To learn more about saving presentations, see section #5.

Note: For this second example, other search phrases you can use to find templates for showcasing images are: **photo album** and **photo collage**. Some phrases like **photos animation** may not yield any results in older versions of PowerPoint. However, searching for the word **pictures** or the word **photos** will produce results in all versions of PowerPoint; the template descriptions can be used to find the best one to suit your needs, with or without animation.

Give it a try!

View Companion Video #2 to see these steps in action

Go to www.youtube.com and search for *#ezppt2*

#3: Simple and Fast Formatting

Important Things to Know About Formatting, Templates and the Slide Master

Before diving into formatting, let's review some important things about templates, the slide master, and master slides. Whether you create a presentation by using a template or from scratch, all presentations have master slides. Master slides are used to control the look of your presentation including fonts, colors, effects, background, and other attributes. You have several options when you begin entering your content in a presentation. *You can:*

- Begin with a template and go with it, making minor edits to formatting as you go.
- Begin with a template and change fonts and other attributes (bold, italics, text effects, etc.) in master slides ahead of time via **View-> Slide Master**.
- Begin with a template, enter all (or most) content and decide later about font and font attributes changes. For example, if you enter content on 20 slides and then decide later that you want to use purple text for all second level text styles, you can edit the font color in the corresponding master slides.
- Begin with a blank presentation, and change fonts and other attributes in the master slides ahead of time; then begin entering content.
- Begin with a blank presentation, formatting and picking slide layouts and styles as you go, and change font and font attributes later (although this option will require the most time and the most decision making).

Remember: If you create a presentation using a template, the font and font attributes used in your slides are based on the default settings in the template. It's a good idea to view the sample slides from a template in slide show mode *first* to decide if you like the fonts and other attributes *before* you start adding a lot of content to your presentation. If you like the font and other attributes in a template, you can proceed with entering your content in the text placeholder boxes. However, if you love the template, but you are not crazy about particular attributes (the font, for example), consider editing the font in the **Slide Master** first. This will save you time in the long run. You can still edit the font and other attributes later; however, if you change a font, for example, in the **Slide Master** *first*, then when you use that master slide layout, the font will already be changed for you as you customize your presentation.

If you create a presentation from scratch, there are still a series of master slides available that you can customize before you enter all your content. Recommendation: Begin by entering some text on one or two slides and test out your slide show. If there are formatting attributes that you want to change for all slides, apply the changes to the **Slide Master** at that point, before you enter the rest of your content.

To review the slide layouts in the Slide Master for your presentation, click **View-> Slide Master**. To learn more about the **Slide Master** and how to make global formatting changes, see section #6 in this book entitled **Using the Slide Master**.

Text Selection Tricks

Before applying any formatting (including font, font size, font color, bold, italics, underline, etc.), select the text to be formatted. There are many ways to select text. Did you know you can use your mouse as well as your keyboard to select your text?

Selecting Words and Paragraphs Using Your Mouse:

- To select a text range, point your mouse and drag; release your mouse to end the selection.
- To select one word, double-click while pointing to the word with your mouse.
- To select a paragraph, triple-click while pointing anywhere in the paragraph.

Selecting Text Using Your Keyboard:

- To select text left to right, click on the starting point, then press **SHIFT + right arrow** to select text.
- To select right to left, click on the starting point, then press **SHIFT + left arrow** to select text.
- To select all text in a particular text box, press **CTRL + A** (Select All).

Applying Formatting Using the Ribbon

Once the text to be formatted is selected, one way to select formatting options is via the **Home** tab. In the **Ribbon**, click on the desired icon in the **Font** group:

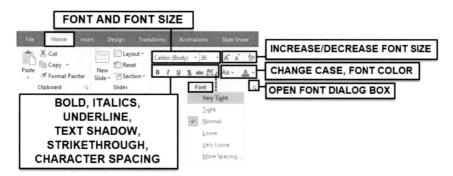

Notice that some font attributes only require one click of the mouse including bold, italics, underline, text shadow, and strikethrough. Some of these commands also have keyboard shortcuts: **CTRL + B** for bold, **CTRL + I** for italics, and **CTRL + U** for underline.

Some font attributes contain a drop-down menu to select from including font, font size, character spacing, change case and font color.

To view all font options, click on the diagonal arrow on the bottom right of the **Font** group to open the **Font** dialog box.

Applying Formatting Using the Shortcut Menu

After selecting text, a shortcut menu displays. It includes some font attributes as well as some paragraph formatting options.

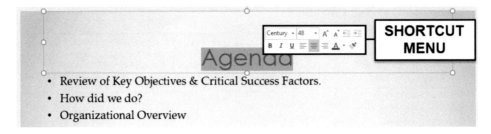

The font shortcut menu disappears once you move the mouse away from the selected text. You can bring the shortcut menu back by right-clicking on your selected text. Doing so displays yet another menu, with even more options. From the right-click menu, you can also click on "**Font…**" (that's the word "**Font**" with the ellipsis after it) to display the **Font** dialog box.

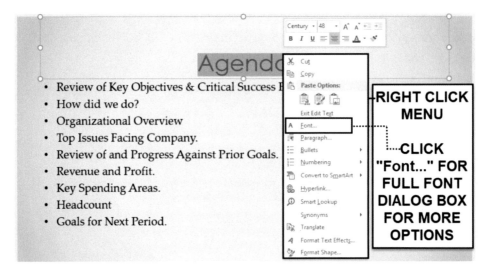

View Companion Video #3 to see these steps in action

Go to www.youtube.com and search for ***#ezppt3***

#4: Copy/Paste Tricks and the Format Painter

As you enter content on your slides, you may need to either duplicate or move text or objects to a new location on the same slide, or to other slides. At times, you may find yourself spending a lot of time formatting one slide and wishing there was an easy way to magically duplicate the formatting (but not the text) from one slide to another. There *is* a way! By using the format painter.

Before we talk about the Format Painter, let's review some tips, tricks, and shortcuts for copying and pasting as well as cutting and pasting. If you've read my other books, you may know that I like to try to figure out the fastest ways to execute commands. Therefore, I've listed a number of methods below, from slowest to fastest, including some keyboard shortcuts.

First, select what you need to copy or cut. Just like when you apply formatting, first, you'll need to select the text or objects which you need to duplicate (copy and paste) or move (cut and paste). You can follow the same text selection tricks covered in section #3 in this book to select your text. Once you've selected your text or objects, continue with the copy, cut, and paste instructions below.

4 Ways to Copy Selected Text or Objects

To copy text or objects, do one of the following:

- **Copy Option #1**: From the Home tab in the ribbon, click **Copy.**
- **Copy Option #2**: Right-click and select **Copy.**
- **Copy Option #3**: Press **CTRL + INSERT.**
- **Copy Option #4**: Press **CTRL + C.**

3 Ways to Cut Selected Text or Objects

To move text or objects, do one of the following:

- **Cut Option #1**: From the **Home** tab in the ribbon, click **Cut**.
- **Cut Option #2**: Right-click and select **Cut**.
- **Cut Option #3**: Press **CTRL+X**.

The Many Ways to Paste

Before pasting, if you are pasting to a slide other than the current slide, navigate to the destination slide where you want to move your text and objects. To paste the text or objects which you have copied or cut, there are multiple options.

Paste Option #1 (Using the Ribbon): From the **Home** tab in the **Ribbon**, click on the drop-down arrow under **Paste**. There you will find four paste options.

- **Use Destination Theme** (paste using the current format)
- **Keep Source Formatting** (paste using the original format)
- **Picture** (paste as an image)
- **Keep Text Only** (paste text only, and don't carry over any formatting)

For additional options, click **Paste Special** to open the **Paste Special** dialog box.

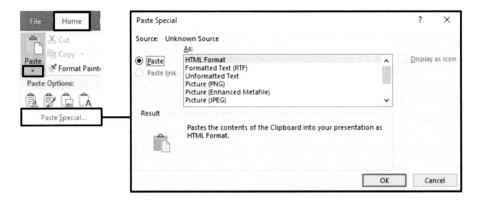

In the **Paste Special** dialog box, you can paste as **HTML Format**, **Rich Text Format** (RTF), **Unformatted Text**, and various image format options including **PNG**, **JPG**, **GIF,** and **BMP**.

The **Paste link** radio button (which is dim in the image above) becomes available if you are pasting a hyperlink.

Paste Option #2 (Using the Right-Click):

- Right-click anywhere on your slide.
- The right-click menu displays. The same four paste options listed above are also available in the right-click menu. Select a paste option as needed. This saves you a little time as compared to executing these commands in the Ribbon.

Note: These four additional Paste options are not available in PowerPoint 2007.

Paste Option #3 (Using the Keyboard):

To quickly paste, use one of following keyboard shortcuts:

- Press **CTRL+V**, or;
- Press **SHIFT+INSERT**.

Note: When pasting via keyboard shortcuts, although this method is the fastest, it defaults to the **Paste** option, **Keep Source Formatting**. If you need specific **Paste** options, refer to the other **Paste** commands in Option #1 and #2 above.

The Format Painter

Now, let's talk about the **Format Painter**, which is the little paintbrush icon on the Home tab. This nifty tool allows you to quickly apply the same formatting such as color, font size, image edge effect, etc. from one area of your presentation to another. This includes both text and graphic formatting. So, if you like the look and formatting of your presentation in one area, you can apply that look to other content in your presentation.

To use the Format Painter:

1. Click on the text or object which contains the formatting you would like to copy.
2. Click the **Format Painter** icon. A paintbrush displays next to your mouse pointer (I-beam).
3. Position your mouse pointer (which shows the little paintbrush symbol) to the text or graphic to apply the formatting, and then either click to apply the formatting to one word or object; or click and drag to *paint* over a large area of text or objects to apply formatting across a large area.

Quick Trick!

Note: Need to apply the same formatting to multiple places on your slide or slides, or even in another presentation? Instead of single clicking on the Format Painter icon, double-click instead. The little paintbrush which displays next to your mouse pointer will remain so that you can apply formatting and keep clicking to apply formatting to additional areas of your presentation. If you jump to a new slide, you may need to double-click to apply formatting in a separate text box. Press the Escape (ESC) key when you're finishing using the Format Painter.

View Companion Video #4 to see these steps in action

Go to www.youtube.com and search for ***#ezppt4***

#5: Opening, Saving, Closing and Printing Presentations

Opening, saving, closing, and printing commands are still accessible through the File menu, but newer versions of Microsoft PowerPoint including PowerPoint 2013 and 2016 offer even more choices when executing these commands. Also, the file menu has changed a bit. Although you can still see the word **File** in the menu bar above the **Ribbon**, once selected, the word **File** disappears from the upper left of the screen.

The **Open** and **Save As** options now display in the right panel, including some new options:

- **Recent** – Select from a list of recent files.
- **One Drive** – Access OneDrive (requires a login) to access or save your files via cloud-based storage.
- **This PC*** – Select from a list of files from your local C: drive (default location: Documents folder).
- **Add a Place** – Add locations for cloud-based storage.
- **Browse** – Display the familiar **Open** or **Save As** dialog box (**Computer-> Browse** in PowerPoint 2013).

*The option in the **File-> Open** and **File-> Save** menu entitled **This PC** is new in PowerPoint 2016.

The **File** menu in newer versions of PowerPoint has some additional menu features including:

- **Info** - for Protection, Inspection, and Management options.
- **Share** - for easy ways to share with others via email, blog, or online; or publish to a slide library or Sharepoint site.
- **Export** - to create PDF/XPS files or other file types, videos, CD presentation packages, or handouts.
- **Account** - for accessing your Microsoft account options.
- **Feedback** - to provide feedback to Microsoft.
- **Options** - originally the PowerPoint Options button, for setup of global options.
- **Add-ins** - for additional Add-ins installed in your version.

Let's get back to the **Open**, **Save**, **Close,** and **Print** commands. Other than the **File** menu, another way to execute these commands is via keyboard shortcuts:

- **CTRL+O** = Open
- **CTRL+S** = Save (If you haven't saved your file yet, Save As options display)
- **CTRL+W** = Save and Close (This option saves and then immediately closes your presentation; if you haven't saved your file yet, a prompt displays asking you if you want to Save, Don't Save or Cancel)
- **CTRL+P** = Print

Printing Options

Although most PowerPoint presentations are viewed in a digital fashion, either online or in person via a projector, there may be times you need to print your presentation, handouts, or notes. After selecting to print via **File-> Print** or the keyboard shortcut **CTRL + P**, you may see a different Print options screen depending on the version of PowerPoint you are using.

In older versions of PowerPoint, the familiar **Print** dialog box displays. In newer versions of PowerPoint including 2013 and 2016, print options display in a pane on the left, as shown in the image below.

If you don't change a thing, PowerPoint will use the default options as listed below to print your presentation. However, you can make changes including slide selections and color options:

Note: PowerPoint 2016 is shown above; in older versions of PowerPoint (2007), click **File→ Print→ Preview→ Page Setup** for all print options. Some options may vary in different versions of PowerPoint.

If you're ready to print, click the **Print** button (click **OK** in older versions of PowerPoint).

To print more than one copy, change the number in the **Copies** field.

Your default **Printer** will show; change as needed. Click **Printer Properties** for additional options specific to your printer.

Settings:

Print All Slides: All slides will print by default. Click the drop-down for additional options including Print Selection (to select specific slides, return to your slides, then hold the CTRL key down to select slides before you print), **Print Current** slide (only print current slide) or **Custom Range** (enter specific slides to print; this positions your cursor in the Slides field below).

Slides: To print specific slides, enter the slide numbers (1,3) or slide range (2-5).

Full Page Slides: Options include **Full Page Slides**, **Notes Pages**, **Outline**, **Handouts** (1 Slide, 2 Slides, 3 Slides, 4, 6 or 9 Slides Horizontal, 4, 6 or 9 Slides Vertical), **Frame Slides** (adds a thin black frame), **Scale to Fit Paper**, **High Quality**, **Print Comments** and **Ink Markup**.

Collated: It will automatically collate, or you can choose not to collate.

Color: Select Color, Grayscale, or Pure Black and White.

View Companion Video #5 to see these steps in action

Go to www.youtube.com and search for *#ezppt5*

Part II: *Working with the Slide Master*

Contents

Working with the Slide Master

* Template - "save as" → Powerpoint Template
* New layout =
    - Slidemaster Tab
    - Insert placeholder

#6: Using the Slide Master

What is the Slide Master Used For?

The **Slide Master** and its associated layout slides serve a dual purpose: they control the attributes, design, and layout of your slides, and they house text and objects which may need to appear on every slide or some slides. The amount of layout slides in a Slide Master varies based on the selected template. The **Slide Master** is located in the **Master Views** group in the **View** tab.

When you need to change the font, font size, font color, and other attributes, are you making the changes on multiple slides? You could use the **Format Painter** for minimal changes, but if you need to make global changes to all slides, there's an easier way – use the **Slide Master**.

When you need to place a logo, graphic, or footer text on every slide, don't waste time trying to copy the text or object on every slide – instead, use the **Slide Master**.

First, let's review how to access the **Slide Master**. From any slide, click **View-> Slide Master**.

After accessing the **Slide Master**, the **Slide Master** tab is available:

From the Slide Master tab you can:
- ➤ **Insert a new Slide Master** – insert a new collection of master slides
- ➤ **Insert Layout** – insert a new layout slide within the current **Slide Master**
- ➤ **Delete, Rename, or Preserve** – delete or rename the current master slide; preserve the current master with the presentation even if it is not used (latter is dim unless you click on the top master slide)

- **Master Slide** – choose the elements to include in the slide master (click on the top slide first)
- **Insert Placeholder** – add a placeholder (picture, table, media, or text) to the current master slide
- **Title and Footers** (checkboxes) – show or hide the **Title** placeholder or **Footer** placeholders on this slide
- **Themes** – Edit or change the theme for the current **Slide Master**
- **Background group (Colors, Text, Effects, and Background)** – change theme attributes or background styles
- **Slide Size** – change the size of the slides in your presentation (In PowerPoint 2007 and 2010, options include **Page Setup** and **Slide Orientation** options
- **Close Master View** – return to your slide show (exit from the master slides view)

How Do I Make Changes Using the Slide Master?

Scenario #1: Let's say you need to change the theme colors as well as the font on all slides in your presentation. From the **Slide Master** view, in the **Background** group on the **Slide Master** tab, click the drop-down for **Colors**, and select a new color theme. **Note**: In PowerPoint 2007 and 2010, **Colors** can be found in the **Edit Theme** group.

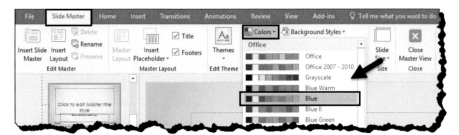

Next, click the drop-down for **Fonts**, and select a **Font**.

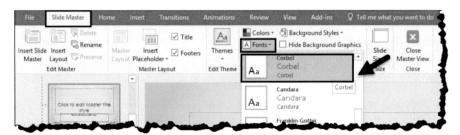

The new color theme and font will then be changed and reflected on all slides in your presentation.

Scenario #2: Let's say you want your company logo in the same location on every slide.

1. From the **Slide Master** view, use the vertical scrollbar to move to the top of the thumbnails; click on the top thumbnail image to select the **Slide Master**. Doing so ensures that the logo image you insert will appear on every slide. If you select a layout slide and not the top slide in the **Slide Master**, then the image will only be inserted on that particular layout slide, and therefore will only appear in your slide show when that particular layout slide is selected as a layout.
2. Click **Insert-> Pictures,** navigate to the location of your logo image, and insert it in one of two ways: double-click on the image or single click on the image and then click **Open**. You will immediately see the image on all the slide layout thumbnails in the **Slide Master**. Press and drag the image to reposition it. To resize the image, point to one of the corner handles (not the side handles) and drag inward to downsize or outward to increase the size.
3. Return to your slide show by selecting **View-> Normal**.
4. At this point, you should see the logo image on every slide in your presentation. If you need to resize or change the logo, return to the **Slide Master** to make the change.

How Do You Use the Different Slide Layouts From the Slide Master in Your Presentation?

Whether or not you make changes to the slides in the **Slide Master**, when you insert slides into your presentation, you're using slide layouts from the **Slide Master**. Let's review the slides in the **Slide Master**. There's the main slide in **Slide Master** – which is the slide at the very top – and then there are a series of layout slides. Each of the layout slides has a unique layout, which contains a different amount of placeholders, including text placeholders, picture/object placeholders, and footer placeholders.

If you make a change to the **Slide Master**, the change affects all other related layout slides. Scenarios #1 and #2 on the previous page demonstrated how to make global changes in your slide show using the **Slide Master**.

If you make a change to a layout slide other than the top slide in the **Slide Master**, then the change only applies to that specific layout slide. Let's make a change to a specific layout slide. Then we'll return to Normal view to see how it all works.

In the image below, the **Slide Master** was accessed via **View-> Slide Master**. By hovering over any thumbnail, the name of the layout slide displays. For example, the fourth thumbnail in the Slide Master pictured below is entitled **Section Header Layout**. The text color in the text placeholder on this particular layout slide has already been changed to red. Now, whenever the **Section Header Layout** is selected as the layout for any slides in the slide show, the text color in this particular placeholder will be red.

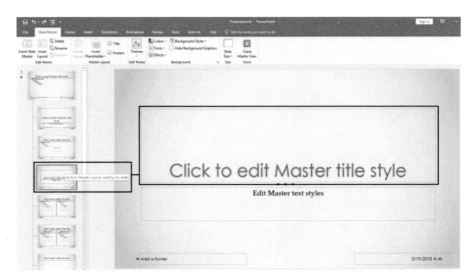

Next, to return to the slide show, click **View-> Normal**.

Let's say you want to apply the **Section Header Layout** (from the Slide Master) to slide 10:

1. In **Normal View**, right click on slide 10 (this selects the slide and displays the right-click menu).
2. From the right-click menu, select Layout. **Note**: You can also select **Layout** from the **Slide** group in the **Home** tab, but selecting it from the right-click menu is faster.
3. From the **Layout** menu, select **Section Header**.

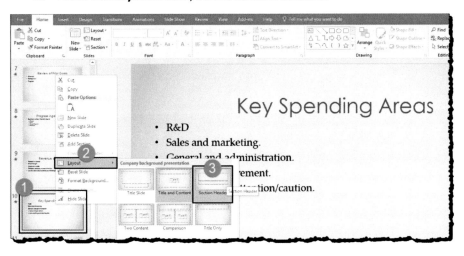

Here's the result:

The **Section Header Layout** is now applied to slide 10, which includes the red text color change made to this layout in the **Slide Master**. Repeat steps 1 to 3 above to apply the layout to other slides as needed.

So, as you can see, the **Slide Master** can be extremely useful for helping you control the attributes and layouts in your slides.

In the next section, you will learn how to use multiple **Slide Masters** within the same presentation, plus a few more tricks.

View Companion Video #6 to see these steps in action

Go to www.youtube.com and search for ***#ezppt6***

when using one template for a # of different uses. Ex: IDEXX Template marketing vs. finance departments

#7: Using Multiple Slide Masters in One Presentation

Let's say your presentation is split up into multiple sections, and you would like each section to have a different theme. Or, what if you need separator slides with a different theme in between various areas of your presentation? How can this be possible if your **Slide Master** contains one theme? This can be accomplished by using multiple Slide Masters. In this example, we'll add a new **Slide Master** and then select a new theme for the additional **Slide Master**.

First, from any slide, click **View-> Slide Master**. Next, do the following:

1. From the **Edit Master** group, select Insert **Slide Master**.
2. A new **Slide Master** – consisting of the main **Slide Master** slide (numbered 2 in the image below) and associated slide layouts – added. Notice there is no theme associated with the new **Slide Master** just yet. We'll come back to that in a moment.
3. The **Preserve** option in the **Edit Master** group is selected (appears in grey) by default. In order to select a theme for our new **Slide Master**, we'll need to toggle the **Preserve** option to **Off**. Click **Preserve**.
4. A prompt appears as follows: "The masters you have chosen not to preserve aren't used by any slides. Do you want PowerPoint to delete these masters?" Select **No**. The **Preserve** option will then be turned off for this new **Slide Master**.

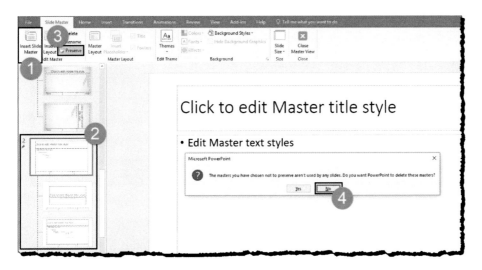

5. Next, from the **Edit Theme** group, click the drop-down arrow for **Themes**.
6. Then select a theme. In this example, the theme entitled "**Gallery**" is selected.

7. The new theme is then applied to the second **Slide Master**.

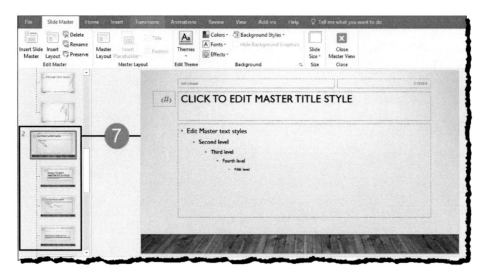

8. Finally, let's apply the second **Slide Master** to some slides in the presentation. Click **View**-> **Normal** to return to your presentation.

9. In this example, let's say you want to apply a layout from the new **Gallery** theme from the new **Slide Master** to slide 4. Right-click on slide 4 to open the right-click menu and select **Layout**.

Quick Tip:

If you want to apply the same layout from your second Slide Master to multiple slides, select multiple slides first by holding the CTRL key down and clicking to select multiple slides. The slides do not have to be in adjacent order. Then right-click while pointing to any of the selected slides and proceed to step 10 below.

10. Notice the available layouts now include the **Gallery** theme layouts from the second **Slide Master**. In this example, the **Section Header** layout is selected.

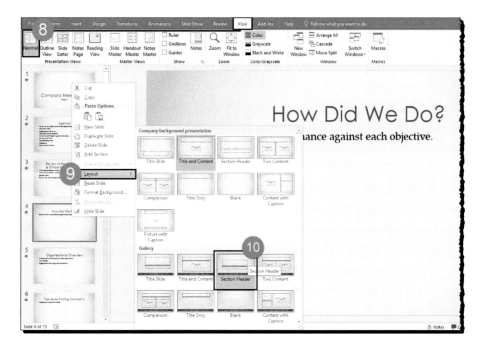

And here's the result:

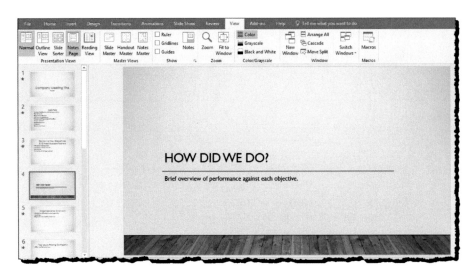

View Companion Video #7 to see these steps in action

Go to www.youtube.com and search for ***#ezppt7***

Part III: *Working with Presentation Slides*

Contents

#8: Inserting, Deleting, Copying, and Moving Slides

If you start with a blank presentation, you'll end up with just one lonely slide in your presentation. On the other hand, if you begin by using a template, you may end up with more slides than you need.

In either case, you'll need to insert, delete, and copy slides at some point while you build your presentation. In **Normal** view, on the pane on the left, click on the appropriate thumbnail for the slide location in your presentation where you would like to either insert, delete, or copy a slide. Then follow the steps below which include several ways to execute each command.

4 Ways to Insert a Slide:

Option #1 – Inserting a Slide Using the Ribbon (1 of 2: Same Layout)

- From the **Insert** tab in the **Ribbon**, in the **Slides** group, click the rectangular icon above **New Slide** to insert a new slide with the same layout as the currently selected slide.

Option #2 – Inserting a Slide Using the Ribbon (2 of 2: Choose a Layout)

1. From the **Insert** tab in the **Ribbon**, in the **Slides** group, click New **Slide** to open the drop-down menu.
2. All available layouts display. Click to select a slide layout.

Option #3 – Inserting a Slide Using the Right-Click Menu (Same Layout)

1. Right-click on the selected slide.
2. Select **New Slide**.

Option #4 – Inserting a Slide Using a Keyboard Shortcut (Same Layout)

- Using your keyboard, press **CTRL + M** to insert a new slide with the same layout as the currently selected slide.

Quick Tip – Choosing a New Layout:

To choose a new layout for an existing slide, right-click on the slide and select Layout to choose a new slide layout. You can also select a layout using the Ribbon via the Home tab: click Layout in the Slides group.

3 Ways to Delete a Slide:

Option #1 – Deleting a Slide Using the Right-Click Menu

- Right-click on the slide to be deleted and click Delete Slide.

Option #2 – Deleting a Slide (Alternate Method Using Cut)

- Another way to delete a slide is by selecting Cut either from the right-click menu, or from the Clipboard group in the Home tab.

Option #3 – Deleting Slides Using a Keyboard Shortcut

- With the slide selected, press the **Delete** key on your keyboard. *This is by far the fastest way to delete a slide.*

Quick Tip – Deleting Multiple Slides:

To delete multiple slides in one sweep, hold the CTRL key down and click to select multiple adjacent or non-adjacent slides; then press the Delete key or use any of the other methods above to delete the slides. If you have a range of adjacent cells to delete (for example, let's say you need to delete slides 6 through 10), click on the first slide in the range; then hold the SHIFT key down and click on the last slide in the range; once the range of slides is selected, just press the Delete key or use one of the methods above to delete the slides.

3 Ways to Copy or Duplicate a Slide

What's the Difference between Copy and Duplicate? If you copy a slide, it places a copy of the slide on the clipboard so you can paste it elsewhere. If you duplicate a slide, it will copy the slide as is and place a duplicate of the slide in the next slide position. Before you begin, remember that you can select one slide or multiple slides; after selecting the first slide, **CTRL + click** to select additional non-adjacent slides or **SHIFT + click** to select a range.

Option #1 – Copying or Duplicating a Slide Using the Ribbon

1. From the **Clipboard** group in the **Home** tab of the **Ribbon**, click **Copy**; or, to **Duplicate** the slide, click on the drop-down arrow next to **Copy** and select **Duplicate**.
2. If you select **Copy**, click in the destination location to paste the copied slide; then click a **Paste** option from the **Paste** drop-down in the **Clipboard** group (Use **Destination Theme**, **Keep Source Formatting**, or **Picture**). You can also select a **Paste** option from the right-click menu.

Option #2 – Copying or Duplicating a Slide Using the Right-Click Menu

1. Right-click on the slide to be copied or duplicated; click **Copy** or **Duplicate**.
2. If you select **Copy**, click in the destination location to paste the copied slide; then right-click and select a **Paste** option (**Use Destination Theme**, **Keep Source Formatting**, or **Picture**).

Option #3 – Copying or Duplicating a Slide Using a Keyboard Shortcut

Using your keyboard, press **CTRL + C** to copy a new slide. Next, click on the destination location to paste the copied slide; then press **CTRL + V** (or **SHIFT + INSERT**). To duplicate a slide using your keyboard, press **CTRL + D**.

4 Ways to Move Slides

You can move one slide or several slides at a time. After selecting the first slide, **CTRL + click** to select additional non-adjacent slides or **SHIFT + click** on another slide to select a range.

Option #1 – Moving a Slide Using the Ribbon (Via Cut and Paste)

1. From the **Clipboard** group in the **Home** tab of the **Ribbon**, click **Cut**.
2. Click on the destination location; then click a **Paste** option from the **Paste** drop-down in the **Clipboard** group (**Use Destination Theme, Keep Source Formatting**, or **Picture**). You can also select a **Paste** option from the right-click menu.

Option #2 – Moving a Slide Using the Right-Click Menu (Via Cut and Paste)

1. Right-click on the selected slide (if you selected more than one slide, you can right-click on any selected slide) and select **Cut**.
2. Right-click on the destination location; select a **Paste** option from the right-click menu (**Use Destination Theme, Keep Source Formatting**, or **Picture**).

Option #3 – Moving a Slide Using a Keyboard Shortcut

1. Using your keyboard, press **CTRL + X**. This removes the slide from the current location and places it on the clipboard so you can paste it elsewhere.
2. Click in the destination location to paste (move) the slide; then press **CTRL + V** (or **SHIFT + INSERT**).

Option #4 – Moving a Slide Using the Mouse (Fastest Method)

This method allows you to use your mouse to press and drag slides to rearrange them. Click the thumbnail for the slide you want to move; then drag it to the new location. That's all there is to it! You can also select multiple slides (**CTRL + click** to select multiple slides or **SHIFT + click** to select a range); then drag the slides to a new location.

View Companion Video #8 to see these steps in action

Go to www.youtube.com and search for *#ezppt8*

Part IV: *Backgrounds, Objects, Images, and Media*

Contents

Backgrounds, Objects, Images, and Media

Colors and Backgrounds

Text Boxes and Shapes

Working with Pictures

Inserting Media (Video, Audio, and Screen Recording)

#9: Colors, Themes, and Backgrounds

To change the color background for one slide or all slides:

1. Right-click on the slide thumbnail or on the slide itself.
2. Select **Format Background**. You can also select **Format Background** from the **Design** tab in the **Ribbon**. **Note**: In PowerPoint 2007 and 2010, from the **Design** tab, click **Background Styles**-> **Format Background**.
3. Beginning in PowerPoint 2013, a **Format Background** pane opens on the right. In earlier versions of PowerPoint, a **Format Background** dialog box displays. In **Fill** options, click the **Solid fill** radio button.
4. To change the default color, click the drop-down arrow for **Color** and select a different color from the palette, or click **More Colors** for more options. To select a specific color from an image, select **Eyedropper**; then point to a color on any image and click to select the color. **Note**: Eyedropper is only available in PowerPoint 2013 and higher.
5. Finally, to save your new color background selection, you have two options:
    - **Option #1**: Click **X** on the upper right of the **Format Background** pane to apply the change to the current slide (in earlier versions of PowerPoint, click **Close**); or
    - **Option #2**: Click **Apply to All** to apply the color change to all slides.

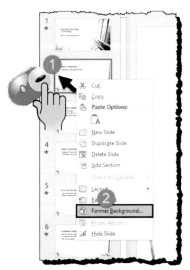 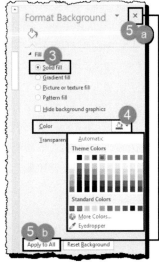

To change the color theme for all slides:

In section #6, you learned how to change the color theme using the **Slide Master**. Another option is to pick an alternate color theme from the **Design** menu. This changes the color scheme as well as the theme for all slides. Here's how:

1. From any slide, click the **Design** tab.
2. Then click on an alternate theme.

Note: Ideally, it's best to change a design theme before you begin entering all your content. This is because when you change a design theme, text and objects may be adjusted with regards to size and placement on your slide; this is due to where placeholders are located on the individual slide layouts in the template.

As a rule of thumb:

- Try experimenting with different templates first to narrow down the best one to suit your needs, before adding a lot of text and images.
- Enter sample text on just a few slides to make sure the selected template will align with your content.
- If you decide to change a design theme, make a backup copy of your file first, just in case too many changes occur in the transition. You can also click **Undo (CTRL+Z)** to undo your changes after you apply a new design, if you change your mind.
- Don't forget about the **Slide Master** when using templates; you can customize slides including template layouts by making changes in the **Slide Master**. If you need more help with the **Slide Master**, refer to section #6 in this book.

Summary of All Format Background Options

In addition to changing the background color and design theme, there are additional formatting options for your slide backgrounds including **Gradient fill**, **Picture or texture fill**, and **Pattern fill**.

From any slide, right-click on a slide and select **Format Background**, or click **Format Background** from the **Design** tab in the **Ribbon.**

Format Background options are available in the pane on the right in PowerPoint 2013 and higher. In earlier versions of PowerPoint, the options are available in the **Format Background** dialog box.

Fill Options:

- **Solid Fill** – Select a solid color for your background (this is explained at the beginning of this section).
- **Gradient Fill** options:
    - **Preset Gradient** - Select a pre-selected gradient color scheme by selecting **Preset Gradients** and then select **Type** and **Direction**.
    - **Gradient Stops** - Customize your gradient background by selecting **Gradient Stops**. Pick a color for the first and last **Gradient stop** (there are two stops by default); you can add additional colors by selecting **Add Gradient Stop** and picking an additional color. **Note**: If you don't see the gradient effect right away, click on another theme and then click back on your current theme to see the effect.
    - **Other Gradient Options** – After selecting your **Preset Gradient** or custom **Gradient Stops**, adjust the **Position, Transparency,** and **Brightness** if needed.

- **Picture or Text Fill** – Select a picture to insert as the background or click the drop-down arrow for texture to select a texture option. There are also **Transparency**, **Alignment**, and **Mirror** options.

View Companion Video #9 to see these steps in action

Go to www.youtube.com and search for *#ezppt9*

#10: Text Boxes, Text Placeholders, and Shapes

Text Boxes vs. Text Placeholders

Whether you start with a blank presentation or a template, there's a pretty good chance the slide you are working on has at least one text placeholder. A text placeholder is different from a text box. First, let's look at some examples of text placeholders.

If you begin with a blank presentation, the first slide contains two text placeholders as shown below, including a title placeholder in large font and a subtitle placeholder in a smaller font.

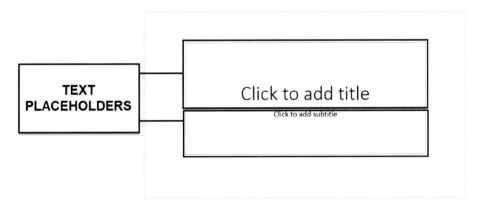

If you begin with a template, the first slide also contains two text placeholders. However, the formatting of the text will vary with regards to font, style, and color based on the selected template.

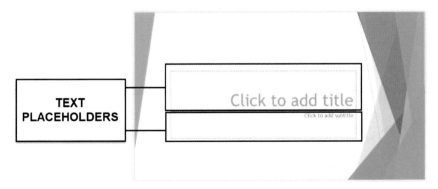

Text placeholders originate from the different layouts in the **Slide Master** and can *only* be added in the **Slide Master**. They contain temporary text prompts

57

such as "Click to add title." The text prompts do not show in a slide show. To add text in a text placeholder, just click inside and start typing. If you delete text in a text placeholder, your text disappears, but the text placeholder remains. To delete the text placeholder altogether, click on the edge of the text placeholder (the dotted line changes to a solid line), and press the **Delete** key.

Text boxes, on the other hand, can be added anywhere on any slide. However, the difference is that the text box only remains if there is text inside the box; whereas a text placeholder remains unless you delete the placeholder itself.

To Insert a Text Box:

1. From the **Insert** tab on the **Ribbon**, select **Text Box** from the **Text** group.
2. Move your cursor anywhere on your slide. Notice that your mouse pointer now shows a vertical line with a small horizontal line on the bottom half as shown in the image below.

3. Move to the location where you want to add the text box; then press and drag using your mouse to draw your box. Release the mouse when you are finished drawing the box.
4. A text box is then added for you to enter text. If you don't enter text in your new text box and you click outside of the box, the text box disappears. If you enter text but then delete the text later, the text box is also removed.

How to Move Text Placeholders, Text Boxes, or Other Shapes

Text placeholders, text boxes, or shapes can be moved easily by using your mouse. Here's how:

1. Click on any edge of a text box until handles appear in the corner. **Note**: Handles vary depending on the version of PowerPoint you are using. For example, in PowerPoint 2016, handles appear as small circles. In earlier versions of PowerPoint, such as 2007 and 2010, corner handles display as circles and midpoint handles display as small squares.
2. Grab hold of the box by pointing to any part of the line border until a four-headed arrow displays. **Note**: Do not point to a handle when moving a text box or placeholder (a double-headed arrow displays); doing so will resize your text box rather than allow you to move the entire box.
3. Press and drag the box to any location on the slide; release to dock the placeholder, text box, or other object.

Note: To move a text placeholder, text box, or shape to another slide, click to select the object, then select **Cut** (**CTRL + X** for example) to remove the box from the current location. Then navigate to the new location and select **Paste** (**CTRL+ V** for example). To remove it altogether, just select it and then use either **Cut** or **Delete**.

How to Add Color and Style to your Text Box, Text Placeholder, or Shape

Text boxes default to black text with no outline and no shading. Text placeholders also default to black text with no outline. There may be some variations to color and style depending on the selected template. You can easily add some color and flare. Here's how:

- With the text box selected, do one of the following to access the **Style**, **Fill,** and **Outline** options:
  - **Option #1:** Right-click on the edge of the text box; then click the drop-down arrow for **Style**, **Fill**, or **Outline** and make a selection

(the right-click menu is slightly different in PowerPoint 2007 and 2010 and does not contain **Shape Effects**); or

o   **Option #2:** In the **Format** tab, in the **Shape Styles** group, click on the drop-down arrow for **Quick Styles** or **Shape Effects**, **Shape Fill**, or **Shape Outline** in the **Ribbon**.

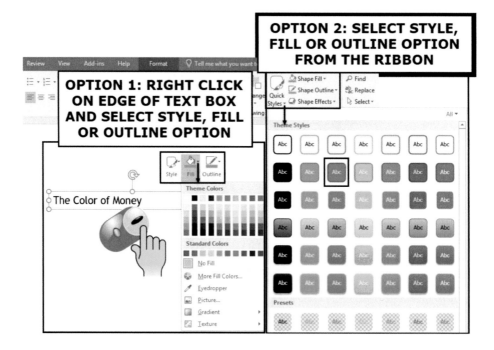

- **Color** options will vary based on the template selected in your presentation. In this example, the **Facet** design template is being used and the dark green **Quick Style** is selected, which includes a green fill color, a darker green outline, and white font color. Here's the result (as compared to the original plain text box in the image above):

The Color of Money

How to Add and Edit a Shape

1. To insert shapes, select one of the following options:

   Option #1:

   From the **Home** tab in the **Ribbon**, in the **Drawing** group, select a shape from the **Recently Used Shapes** shown, or click on the **More** option (the horizontal line with a down arrow) to see all shapes to select from:

   Option #2:

   From the **Insert** tab, in the **Illustrations** group, click **Insert> Shapes**.

   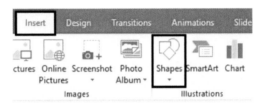

2. Next, a variety of shapes to choose from display including **Recently Used Shapes**, **Lines**, **Rectangles**, **Basic Shapes**, **Block Arrows**, **Equation Shapes**, **Flowchart**, **Stars and Banners**, **Callouts**, and **Action Buttons**. Click to select a shape.

   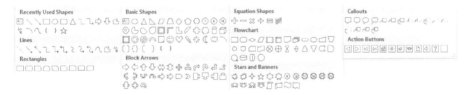

3. Your mouse pointer displays as a cross hair. Click and drag to draw your shape; release your mouse when you are finished drawing your shape. To change the color or style of a shape, refer to the instructions on the previous page on "**How to Add Color and Style to your Text Box, Text Placeholder, or Shape**".

Quick Tip – How to Draw a Symmetrical Shape:

Want to draw a perfect square, circle, or other shape? When drawing a shape, hold the SHIFT key down to draw a symmetrical shape!

How to Add Text to a Shape

1. To add text to a shape, select one of the following options:

   Option #1 (Via the Right-Click Menu):

   Right-click on the shape and select **Add Text**, then start typing. If you return to a shape that already contains text, right-click and select **Edit Text**.

   Option #2 (Faster Method):

With the shape selected, just start typing! A faster way to edit text within a shape if you return back to the shape later is to double-click to select and replace all text, or just single click to insert text in between existing text.

Quick Tip – How to Change a Shape:

*Want to change to a different shape? Double-click on the shape to open the **Format** tab on the **Ribbon**; then from the **Insert Shapes** group, click **Edit Shape** -> **Change Shape**. Click on a different shape to instantly change your shape to a new shape!*

*Want to go a step further and alter particular points of the shape? From the **Insert Shapes** group, click **Edit Shape** -> **Edit Points**. Using your mouse, you can then press and drag in any direction to change the shape at the selected point.*

View Companion Video #10 to see these steps in action

Go to www.youtube.com and search for *#ezppt10*

#11: Working with Pictures, Images, and Symbols

When inserting pictures, you can include photographic images or illustrations from either your local drive or another drive. If you're using PowerPoint 2013 or higher, there's a new feature available in the **Insert** tab in the **Ribbon** called **Online Pictures**. **Online Pictures** allows you to search for a picture via **Bing** or **OneDrive**.

Caution: When inserting any picture in your presentation, be sure to review any copyright rules and regulations. There are various websites which allow you to download pictures for free which follow the Creative Commons license. An example is pixabay.com, which provides images free of charge that you can use for commercial purposes, and no attribution is required.

For a larger variety of pictures and images, websites such as istockphoto.com, thinkstockphotos.com, and gettyimages.com offer subscription services or charge per image.

Once you have your pictures selected, downloaded, and saved, you're ready to insert them in your presentation.

Inserting Images

1. If the slide you are working on has an image placeholder, click on the **Pictures** option, as shown in the image below.

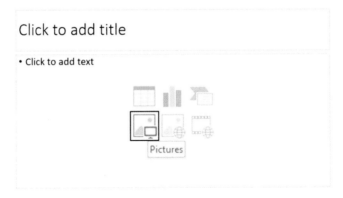

If your slide doesn't have an image placeholder, from the Ribbon, click **Insert**-> **Pictures**.

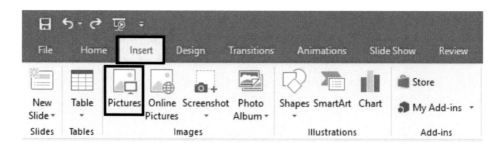

2. Navigate to the location where you have your pictures stored. Then click the picture and select **Insert** (or just double-click on the image).

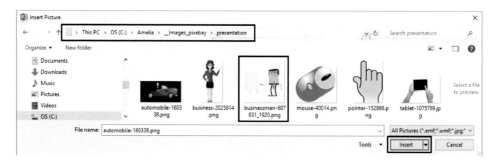

What Can You Do With An Image?

Once your image in inserted, you can:

- **Move the image**: Point to the center of the image, then press and drag to move (your mouse pointer should show a four-headed arrow when moving).
- **Resize the image**: Point to one of the handles in the corner *only*, then while holding the SHIFT key, drag inward or outward to resize. **Note**: Holding the **SHIFT** key retains the aspect ratio. If you take hold of one of the side handles and drag inward or outward, the image will be skewed and misshapen, so I don't usually recommend using the side handles.

- **Format the image**: Double click on the image to open the **Format** tab in the **Ribbon**. From the **Format** tab you can:
    - **Remove the background**: This is especially handy if you need to layer your image over another image and you need to remove the background color (white for instance) or other components of the image. **Note**: This option is not available in PowerPoint 2007.
    - **Make corrections, change the color, or apply artistic effects**: Click the drop-down arrows under **Corrections**, **Color**, or **Artistic Effects** to view available options.
    - **Compress the picture**: Click **Compress Pictures** to select an option to reduce the file size (some options may reduce quality as well).
    - **Change the picture**: Replace the current image with a different image.
    - **Reset the picture**: Discard all the formatting changes you made to the picture.
    - **Add a border or edge effect**: From the **Picture Styles** group, select a border or edge style from the available images; click on the drop-down arrows for **Picture Border**, **Picture Effects,** and **Picture Layout** for even more options. Note: **Picture Shape** changed to **Picture Layout** starting in PowerPoint 2010.
- **Arrange your image**: In the **Arrange** group, there are several options:
    - **Bring Forward** and **Send Background** may be dim if you only have one image, but once you add a second image, the option becomes available so you can select which image you want in the foreground or background.
    - **Selection Pane** opens a **Selection** pane on the right and lets you show or hide images (this is handy when you have several images layered on top of each other).
    - **Align** allows you to align your image to the left or right, etc.
    - **Group** allows you to group selected images together so you can manage them more easily. Grouping images is covered in more detail later in this section.
    - **Rotate** allows you to rotate or flip your image. You can also rotate your image by taking hold of the curved arrow at the top

center of your image and then dragging in a circular motion to rotate manually.

- **Size your image**: In the **Size** group, you can crop your image or change the height or width. To view all **Size** and **Position** options, click the little diagonal arrow on the bottom right of the **Size** group.

Inserting Background Images

There are several ways to consider formatting the background of one or more slides. Here are some suggestions:

Option #1: Format Background

- To add a background color, from the **Design** tab in the **Ribbon**, select **Format background**. This option allows you to add a **Solid Fill**, **Gradient Fill**, **Picture or texture fill,** or **Pattern fill**. You can also choose to hide the background, adjust the transparency, **Apply to All** (to apply the change to all slides), or **Reset the Background**. **Note**: In PowerPoint 2007 and 2010, to access **Format Background** from the **Design** tab, click **Background Styles-> Format Background**.
  - ○ This is an example of what a slide would look like if you applied solid color (the slide below contains one image with a transparent background):

- o This is an example of what an image would look like if you selected **Picture or Texture Fill**-> **Insert picture from**-> **File** and selected a background image:

Option #2: Insert a Background Image

Another way to add a background image is to click **Insert-> Picture** and select an additional image. However, there's one caveat to using this method. The newly added image is inserted in the foreground, and may not extend to the width of the slide. Here's an example of what it may look like:

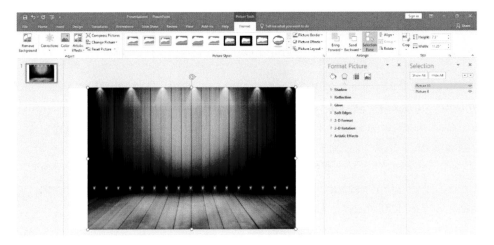

To fix it, you can resize the background and increase the width. I know I said to not use the side handles, but there are some minor exceptions; in this case, dragging the side handles outward will still keep the image looking pretty much the same. Just remember to use the side handles very sparingly.

Where did our little presenter guy go? He's still there but he's in the background. With the newly added image selected, send the image to the back of the slide by right-clicking and select **Send to Back**-> **Send to Back**; or, from the **Format** tab in the **Ribbon**, click **Arrange**-> **Send to Back**.

Here's the result:

Option #3: Insert a Background Image to the Slide Master

Another way to insert a background image is to insert the image in the **Slide Master**. This option is recommended if you are using the same background image for several slides or throughout your whole presentation.

If you are adding a background image to a particular slide layout (to reuse within your presentation), before accessing the slide master, check to see which layout is used for your current slide (so you know which layout to add the background image to when you are in the **Slide Master**); just right click on the slide thumbnail (if you don't see thumbnails, click **View**-> **Normal**) and select **Layout**. The layout used by the selected slide (**Title Slide**, **Title and Content**, etc.) will be highlighted in grey.

To add a background image to the **Slide Master**:

1. Click **View-> Slide Master. Note**: When you access the **Slide Master**, the **Slide Master** tab becomes available.
2. If you want to add a background image for *all* slides, click on the uppermost top slide in the **Slide Master**. If you only want to add a background image to a particular slide layout, then click on the desired slide layout thumbnail (**Title Slide, Title and Content**, etc.). **Note**: The slide layout shows when you hover over each slide thumbnail with your mouse. You can see an example in the image in step 4 below.
3. Next, click on the **Slide Master** tab in the **Ribbon** (it may already be selected); in the **Background** group, click the drop-down arrow next to **Background Styles**. Beneath the list of colored backgrounds, click **Format Background** for additional options. Here, you will find the **Format Background** options including **Solid Fill, Gradient Fill, Picture or Texture Fill, Pattern Fill, Transparency, Apply to All,** and **Reset the Background**).
4. Let's say in this case, you want to apply a business background image (which you have saved on your local drive) to just the **Title Slide** layout. Click on the **Title Slide** layout (which is the second slide in the image below); then click **Background Styles-> Format Background**. The **Format Background** pane displays on the right (note that the pane is new in PowerPoint 2013 and higher; prior versions will display a dialog box instead). Select the **Picture or texture fill** option on the right (or select via a dialog box in older versions of PowerPoint); click **File** and then select your background image.

5. To return back to your presentation, click **View->Normal**. The background image should now appear on your slide, which is using the **Title Slide** layout. Now, every time you insert a new slide with the **Title Slide** layout, the new background image will already be applied to the

slide! This is the advantage to using the **Slide Master**. If you decide to change the background image of the **Title Slide** layout, it can only be changed in the **Slide Master**. To see a demonstration of all steps, refer to the link at the end of this section to view the companion video.

Overlaying and Combining Text and Graphics

Once you add an image or two, it's time to add some text to your slide. It's easy to add text and overlay it on your image. Click **Insert->Text Box**. Draw your text box and enter your text. It should already be overlaid on top of your graphics (it will default to the **Foreground** position). Format your text as needed. See section #10 in this book for more information about formatting text boxes. That's all there is to it! Here's an example of how it might look:

Grouping Objects

If you have a lot of objects on a slide, including images, text boxes, and shapes, it may be helpful to group objects together. This makes it easy to move or copy multiple objects at the same time. To group objects on a slide, you'll need to select all the objects you want to group.

- Click on the first object, then hold the **SHIFT** key down and click to select additional objects.
- If you want to select all objects on a slide, click **CTRL + A** to **Select All**. To unselect an object, hold the **CTRL** key down and click to deselect.
- Once all the objects you wish to group are selected, right-click while pointing to any of the selected objects; then select **Group-> Group**.

Your objects are now grouped together in one object which can be easily moved or copied. To ungroup objects, click to select the grouped object, right-click and select **Group-> Ungroup**.

Quick Tip – Inserting Symbols, Icons – Secret Little Pictures!

*Do you need a quick symbol or icon in a snap? Did you know there are hundreds of little symbols and icons available in the **Symbols** option in the **Insert** tab? First, insert a text box (otherwise **Symbols** will be greyed out); then click **Insert-> Symbols** and select **Webdings** or **Wingdings** in the **Font** drop-down menu. Next, click on a symbol, then click **Insert-> Close**. These fonts contain all kinds of little symbols and icons, and even a variety of pictures to choose from. These symbols are considered characters, so they're not shapes. Although you can't apply the same formatting you can with **Shapes**, you can change the appearance of a symbol the same way you would format text. First, select the symbol the same way you select text, then change the font size or color, or apply attributes such as bold, italics, or text effects. **Format Text Effects** is available if you right click on a symbol, or via the **Format** tab in the **Ribbon**. Examples of text effects are glow (applied to the palm tree below) or reflection (applied to the yin-yang symbol below). Italicizing a symbol will cause it to slant to the right like the eye symbol below).*

*Here are just a few examples of symbols available in the **Webdings** or **Wingdings** fonts, with some formatting applied:*

View Companion Video #11 to see these steps in action

Go to www.youtube.com and search for ***#ezppt11***

#12: *Inserting Media (Video, Audio, and Screen Recording)*

Ready to make a movie? It's easy to convert your PowerPoint presentation into video format when it's all finished. Beginning in PowerPoint 2013, you can save your slide show to mp4 file format. But first, it's time to add some media to your slide show!

Inserting Video

In the **Ribbon**, from the **Media** group (or the **Media Clips** group in PowerPoint 2007) on the **Insert** tab, click **Video (Movie** in PowerPoint 2007). You have two video options:

- **Online Video**: This option allows you to search for a YouTube video to insert into your presentation or paste the embed code of a website video. If using the YouTube video option, be sure to review and comply with the terms of use policy.
- **Video on My PC**: This option allows you to select a video stored on your local computer. After selecting this option, the **Insert Video** dialog box displays. Navigate and select the video to insert into your presentation. **Note**: The video options varies depending on the version of PowerPoint; earlier versions of PowerPoint prompt to download videos from the web.

Once a video is added to your presentation, a video object displays including a play bar at the bottom of the window.

You can resize the video window on your slide as needed. To remove the video, with the video object selected, press **Delete**.

With the video window selected, a **Playback** tab displays in the **Ribbon**. In the **Playback** tab, you can:

- Play your video.
- Add or remove a bookmark at the current time in the video. The bookmark displays as a dot and will show in the play bar when the video is playing during the slide show.
- Trim your video by specifying the start and end times (via a trim video bar that displays).
- Add a fade effect at the beginning or end of the video.
- Change the volume of the video clip.
- Select Video Options:
  - **Start**: Specify to have the video clip play when clicked or play automatically. If **In Click Sequence** is selected, once video on the first slide is being played, it will play on subsequent slides, or if video is paused, it will be paused on subsequent slides.
  - **Play Full Screen**: Encompass your whole slide while playing the video.
  - **Hide While Not Playing**: Hide the video clip during a slide show if not playing.
  - **Loop until Stopped**: Repeat the video clip until it is stopped.
  - **Rewind after Playing**: Rewind the video clip after it is done playing.
- **Insert Captions**: Insert WebVTT Closed Captions for your video. **Note**: WebVTT is a W3C standard for tracking in HTML5.

Inserting Audio

To insert audio, including voiceover and/or music, from the Media group on the **Insert** tab in the **Ribbon**, click **Audio**. You have two audio options:

Audio on My PC: This option allows you to select recorded audio saved on your computer. After selecting this option, the **Insert Audio** dialog box displays.

— can use bookmark to trigger an animation
Animation — Additional Options
★ Start — With previous — Start w/ play on click)
(or click)

Navigate and select the audio to insert into your presentation and click **Insert**. *Bookmark*
An audio icon along with a play bar displays on your slide.

↓
canthave
video in
full
screen

With the audio icon selected, a **Playback** tab displays in the Ribbon. In the
Playback tab, you can:

— can add
multiple
book-
marks.

- Play your audio.
- Add or remove a bookmark at the current time in the audio. The bookmark displays as a dot and will show in the play bar when the audio is playing during the slide show.
- Trim audio by specifying the start and end times (via a trim audio bar that displays).
- Add a fade effect at the beginning or end of the audio.
- Change the volume of the audio clip.
- Select **Audio Options**:
    - **Start**: Specify to have the audio clip play when clicked or play automatically. If the **In Click Sequence** is selected, once audio on the first slide is being played, it will play on subsequent slides, or if audio is paused, it will be paused on subsequent slides.
    - **Play Across Slides**: Play the audio clip across all slides.
    - **Loop until Stopped**: Repeat the audio clip until it is stopped.
    - **Hide During Show**: Hide the audio clip during a slide show.
    - **Rewind after Playing**: Rewind the audio clip after it is done playing.
- **No Style**: Reset all audio options back to the defaults.
- **Play in Background**: Set the audio clip to continuously play across all slides in the background.

Recording Audio

Did you know you can record audio directly into your PowerPoint presentation? Here's how:

- Click **Insert-> Audio-> Record Audio.**
- The **Record Sound** dialog box displays. Enter a name for your embedded audio.
- Click **Record** (red dot) to begin recording. Click **Stop** (blue square) to stop recording.
- Click **OK** when finishing.

An icon then displays on your slide for your audio clip. The same audio options shown above are then available in the **Playback** tab in the Ribbon. To remove the audio, with the video icon selected, press **Delete**.

Screen Recording

Beginning in PowerPoint 2013, you can record your computer screen and audio as well to insert into your presentation. To record screen activity:

- Click **Insert-> Screen Recording.**
- Your mouse pointer changes into a crosshair. The following options display:

- The **Record** button is dim until you click **Select Area** and select the area to record. Click **Select Area** and then press and drag to select the recording area on your screen.
- You can toggle to record or not record **Audio**, as well as the **Record Pointer** (mouse pointer).

- When you are ready to record, click **Record** (red dot) or press the **Windows key + SHIFT +R**.
- To stop recording, click **Stop**, or press the **Windows key + SHIFT + Q**.

The same video options shown above (in **Insert Video** options) are then available in the **Playback** tab in the Ribbon.

For more info on how to save your slide show to video format, see section #24 in this book.

View Companion Video #12 to see these steps in action

Go to www.youtube.com and search for ***#ezppt12***

Part V: *Slide Show Options*

Contents

Slide Show Options

#13: *Setting Up and Viewing a Slide Show*

While creating your presentation, it's a good idea to test out your slide show and see how it's shaping up. From the **Ribbon**, click the **Slide Show** tab. Let's take a look at the **Slide Show** options:

- **From Beginning**: Start the slide show beginning with your first slide.
- **From Current Slide**: Start the slide show at the current slide.
- **Present Online**: Share your slide show on a web browser using a free Office Presentation service by logging in using a Microsoft account.
- **Custom Slide Show**: Select specific slides to include in a custom slide show.
- **Set Up Slide Show**: Select settings for your slide show including timings, manually advancing slides, looping continuously, options for pen/laser pointer color, slides to include in the slide show, and setting up multiple monitors.
- **Hide Slide**: Hide a particular slide so it won't show during the slide show.
- **Rehearse Timings**: Practice your slide show and record timing for each slide. A prompt displays at the end to ask you if you want to save the timings. **Caution**: If you save the timings, then the timings will be used to automatically advance your slides during your slide show.
- **Record Slide Show**: Specify where to start recording or clear recorded timings and narration. If you saved timings via the **Rehearse Timings** option above, you can clear them here via **Record Slide Show**-> **Clear** -> **Clear Timings on All Slides**.
- **Other Options**: There are also checkboxes to play/not play audio narrations, use timings, show media controls, select a monitor, and use/don't use **Presenter View**.

Start the Show

To View Your Presentation as a Slide Show:

- Click **Slide Show-> From Beginning** (or **Current Slide**). Your slide show begins.

 Quick Tip – Start a Slide Show Instantly

If you want to see your slides in a presentation right away starting at the beginning, just press F5!

If you want to see your slides in a presentation right away starting at the current slide, press SHIFT + F5.

There are numerous ways to navigate your slides while in slide show mode.

5 Ways to Advance Slides During a Slide Show:

- Just press the **N** key on your keyboard, or
- Click your mouse (left mouse button only), or
- Press the Page Down (**PgDn**) key on your keyboard, or
- Press the Down Arrow key on your keyboard, or
- Click your right mouse button, then click **Next**.

4 Ways To Go To A Previous Slide During a Slide Show:

- Just press the **P** key on your keyboard, or
- Press the Page Up (**PgUp**) key on your keyboard, or
- Press the Up Arrow key on your keyboard, or
- Click your right mouse button, then click **Previous** (or press the **P** key on your keyboard).

How to Zoom In During Your Slide Show:

- Click your right mouse button, then click **Zoom** (or press the **Z** key on your keyboard while the right-click menu is displayed).
- Adjust the zoom area by moving your mouse, then click to **Zoom**.
- Press the Escape (**Esc**) key on your keyboard to return to your slide show.

To View Thumbnails or Jump to Another Slide During a Slide Show:

- Click your right mouse button, then click **See All Slides** (or press the **A** key on your keyboard).
- All slides display as small thumbnails. The current slide is shown with a red border and red slide number. From thumbnail mode, you can:
    - o Return to your slide show by either clicking the left arrow in the circle on the upper left, or by pressing the Escape (**Esc**) key on your keyboard.
    - o Jump to another slide by pressing an arrow key on your keyboard and pressing **Enter**, or by clicking on another slide thumbnail.

2 Ways to Exit the Slide Show and Return to Your Slides:

- Press the Escape (**Esc**) key on your keyboard, or
- Click your right mouse button, then click **End Show** (or press the **E** key on your keyboard while the right-click menu is displayed).

Setting Up an Automatic Slide Show

Scenario: You have a booth at a business expo, and you need to run a slide show continuously. How do you set up a slide show to run automatically? Here's how:

1. Once your slide show is completed, do the following to rehearse and record your timings:
    a. Click **Slide Show**-> **Rehearse Timings**.
    b. Go through each slide as you would during your presentation and advance each slide using one of the methods discussed above.

85

c. At the end of the slide show, click **Yes** when prompted to save the new slide timings.

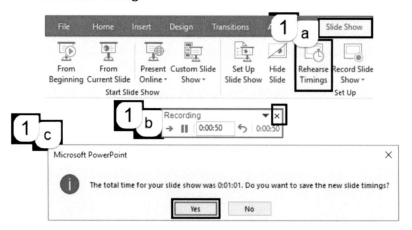

2. Next, to set up your slide show to loop continuously, do the following:
    a. Click **Slide Show**-> **Set Up Slide Show**.
    b. Click in the checkbox to **Loop Continuously until "Esc."**
    c. Make sure the option **Use timings, if present,** is checked.
    d. Click **OK**.

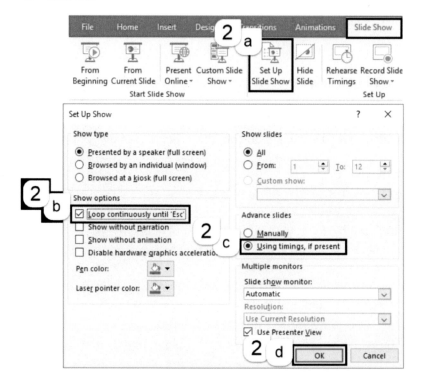

Be sure to test out your automatic slide show by pressing F5. *Your slide show is ready to go!*

Live Presentation with an Electronic Pen and Laser Pointer

Scenario #2: You are presenting your slide show live during a WebEx, and you need the ability to show slide Notes, use the electronic pen in a specific color to draw while you are speaking, use the electronic laser pointer to point out particular parts of a slide, and use the yellow highlighter option (if needed) to emphasize key points. How do you accomplish this? Here's how:

The pen, laser pointer, and highlighter options are available via the right-click menu during a slide show.

Just right-click during a slide show and select **Pointer Options**, then select **Laser Pointer** (shown as the red dot in the image below), **Pen** (see blue circle in the image below), or **Highlighter** (the word "features" on the right in the image below has the **Highlighter** applied).

Select **Ink Color** to change the **Pen** color. In the example below, blue is selected as the **Pen** color.

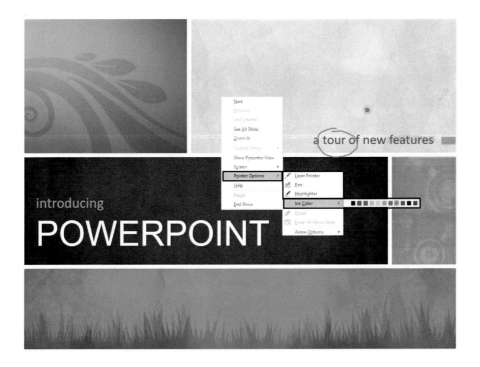

To display **Notes** along with additional options during a slide show, you can use **Presenter View** to accomplish all this. **Presenter View** is designed to work with two monitors: as the presenter, you can view your presentation with **Notes** on one monitor (your laptop, for example), while your audience views the slide show without **Notes** on a second monitor (when projecting on a larger screen, for example).

If you're using one monitor, just press **ALT + F5** to try **Presenter View**.

From inside a slide show, you can toggle to **Presenter View** by right-clicking and selecting **Presenter View**.

Note: In earlier versions of PowerPoint, prior to PowerPoint 2010, **Presenter View** only works if more than one monitor is detected.

Here's an example of a presentation shown in **Presenter View**. Notice that **Notes** display in the pane on the right. There are also slide show options on the bottom left including **Pointer Options**.

View Companion Video #13 to see these steps in action

Go to www.youtube.com and search for **#ezppt13**

#14:   *Running a Slide Show from Your Desktop*

Problem: You're the presenter at a live training session, and you need a quick and easy way to start your presentation so your audience doesn't see you launch your slide show from the **Ribbon** within PowerPoint. How do you accomplish this?

Solution: Save your PowerPoint file as a PowerPoint Show (*.ppsx). This file format will always open in Slide show mode. To run a slide show from your desktop, select the PowerPoint Show (*.ppsx) save option. Here's how**:**

1. Select **File-> Save As**.
2. Click the location where you would like to save your presentation (**Desktop** is suggested for an easy destination to access for launching your slide show).
3. In the **Save As Type** field, select **PowerPoint Show (*.ppsx)**.
4. Click **Save**.

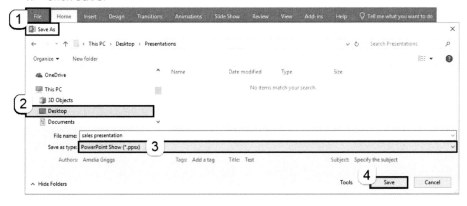

When you're ready to launch your slide show, just double-click the .ppsx file. It will open as a slide show automatically.

Here is a sample presentation ready to be launched from the **Desktop**:

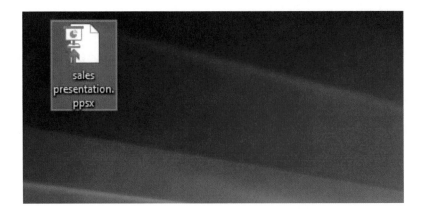

View Companion Video #14 to see these steps in action

Go to www.youtube.com and search for ***#ezppt14***

Part VI: *Animation Station and Special Effects*

Contents

Animation Station and Special Effects

*can set a custom path w/ animations
(scroll to Bottom of animations)*

#15: Entrance, Emphasis, Exit, and Motion Path Animations

It's all about the graphics. Or is it? When selecting graphics, you have the choice of either illustrative graphics or photographic images. But it's not *only* about the graphics – it's *how* the graphics are presented. Which reminds me of that phrase *"Presentation is Everything."*

When your audience views your presentation, will they be wowed? Will they be delighted and amazed? Consider adding a bit of flare to your objects by adding entrance or exit animations, emphasis animations, or motion paths. Just be careful not to add too many animations on a slide. Start with some subtle animations and build from there. Just like a singer reaches a high note at different times in a song, you may want to save the more intense animations for a few special "wow" moments. The amount of animations also depends on the type of presentation you are creating.

There are a multitude of options for each type of animation. Starting in PowerPoint 2010, the variety of animations and the method for applying the animations is much improved. Here's a comparison of animations in PowerPoint 2007 and PowerPoint 2016:

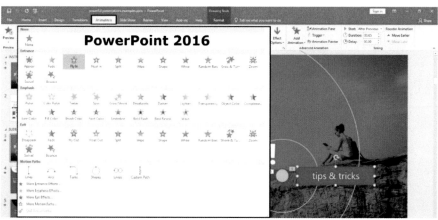

Note: The same animations are available in Microsoft PowerPoint 2010 through 2016.

Starting in PowerPoint 2010, animations are grouped into categories:

- **Entrance Animations** – This type of animation controls how an image or object will initially display on a slide. Examples of entrance animations include: Appear, Fade, Fly In, Float In, Split, Wipe, Shape, Wheel, Random Bars, Grow & Turn, Zoom, Swivel, and Bounce.
- **Exit Animations** – This type of animation controls how an image or object will exit from a slide. Examples of exit animations include: Disappear, Fade, Fly Out, Float Out, Split, Wipe, Shape, Wheel, Random Bars, Shrink & Turn, Zoom, Swivel, and Bounce.
- **Emphasis Animations** – This type of animation is used to emphasize or draw attention to an image or object. Examples of exit animations include: Pulse, Color Pulse, Teeter, Spin, Grow/Shrink, Desaturate, Darken, Lighten, Transparency, Object Color, Complimentary Color, Line Color, Fill Color, Brush Color, Font Color, Underline, Bold Flash, Bold Reveal, and Wave.
- **Motion Paths** – This type of animation is used to apply a motion path to move objects from one position on the screen to another. They are useful when telling a story or explaining a process. Motion path options include Lines, Arcs, Turns, Shapes, Loops, and Custom Path. See sections #20 and #21 in this book for specific examples of motion path animations.
- **More Options**– For even more choices, look under **More Entrance Effects, More Emphasis Effects, More Exit Effects,** and **More Motion Paths**. These options can be found at the bottom of the **More** option or via **Animations-> Add Animation** (see bottom of drop-down options).

*Animation Pane- re-order when each item comes in.

94

Quick Tip – My Favorite Animation Picks

- *My favorite **Entrance** animation for a subtle, professional approach is **Fade**.*
- *My favorite **Entrance** animation for a cool approach is **Float Up**. This animation can be found under **More Entrance Effects**.*
- *My favorite **Entrance** animation for a fun approach is **Bounce**.*
- *My favorite **Emphasis** animation is **Pulse**.*
- *My favorite **Exit** animation is **Float Out**. **Exit** animations for individual images aren't always needed; however, there are exceptions, especially when there is a graphic that needs to make a strong exit. You can also consider **Motion Paths** for Exit animations. For example, let's say you want to show a vehicle riding along a path on the bottom edge of the screen. You can accomplish this by creating a custom **Motion Path**.*
- *As an alternative to Exit animations, you may want to consider a **Slide Transition** instead (that's in the next section #16).*

__Note__: If you are using a version earlier than PowerPoint 2010, animation options may vary.

How to Apply an Entrance, Emphasis, or Exit Animation to an Object

1. Click on an object or element (text, shape, image, etc.) to select it.
2. Click the **Animations** tab.
3. Click to select an **Entrance**, **Emphasis,** or **Exit** animation from the **Ribbon** bar. To see all animations, click **More** (that's the little horizontal line with the down arrow) on the far right of the animations.
4. After selecting the animation, a preview of the animation will be shown. To see the preview again, click **Preview** on the far left of the **Ribbon**. The animation will also be numbered. If this is the first animation applied to the slide, it will be labeled as animation number 1. **Note**: To quickly remove an animation that you *just* applied, click **CTRL + Z** to **Undo**.
5. To change the animation for the selected object, just select a different animation while the object is selected.

6. To add animation to different objects on the same slide, repeat steps 1 to 3. The second animation will be labeled as animation number 2; the third animation will be labeled as animation number 3, and so forth.
7. To add the same animation to multiple objects, hold the **SHIFT** key while clicking to select multiple objects first, and then apply the animation.

To Reorder an Animation:

1. Click on the object containing the animation.
2. From the **Timing** group on the right side of the **Animation** tab in the **Ribbon**, select either **Move Earlier** or **Move Later**.
3. The numbering for the animation then changes for the objects on the given slide.

2 Ways to Remove an Animation

Option #1:

1. Click on the object containing the animation.
2. From the **Animation** tab, click None.
3. The numbering for the animation then disappears, since the object is no longer animated.

Option #2 (An Easier, Faster Way!):

1. Click on the animation number that displays in a little box on your slide. The box changes from white to red.
2. Press **Delete** on your keyboard. That's it! The animation is now removed.

Timing and Animation Triggers:

When you apply an animation, by default it will play when you click on the slide. In the **Animations** tab, this setting is set to **On Click** in the **Timing** group on the right and can be changed to **With Previous** or **After Previous**. These settings are pretty important, because they control when animations occur on your slide.

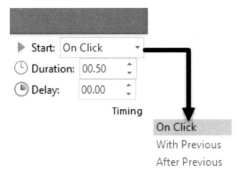

Instead of **On Click**, if you want the animation to occur when the slide displays, change it to **With Previous**. The **After Previous** setting is handy if you have multiple animations occurring on the same slide, and you need a particular animation to occur after another animation is completed.

You can also change the **Duration** of the animation as well as specify an animation **Delay** in the **Timing** group in the **Ribbon**.

You can also apply a **Trigger** to further control when your animations play. **Trigger** is located in the **Advanced Animation** group to the left of the **Timing** group in the **Ribbon**. From the **Trigger** drop-down menu, you can opt to have the animation occur upon clicking on another object, or when media playback reaches a bookmark. Notes: To learn more about adding a bookmark to media, see section #12 in this book.

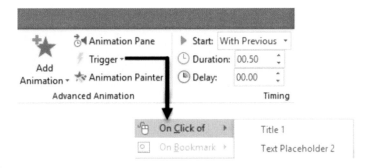

Quick Tip – How Many Animations Per Slide?

When creating animations to add to your presentation, be careful not to apply too many animations on any one given slide. Doing so may not only look unprofessional but may distract the learner from the content being presented. Consider adding animations that enhance the learner experience.

Ask yourself the following questions:
"Does the animation add value to the content or cause a distraction?"
"Will the animation have a positive impact on the content being presented?"
"Does the animation truly improve the learner experience?"

To see a demonstration of how to apply animations to different types of objects – including text boxes, shapes and images – be sure to follow the link below and watch the video!

View Companion Video #15 to see these steps in action

Go to www.youtube.com and search for *#ezppt15*

*Slide sorter view — to reorder slides easily
*can easily add transitions to slides from this view
"*" on Slide = Some kind of animation or transition
on that slide

#16: Slide Transitions

How Are Slide Transitions Different From Animations?

Transitions are applied to *slides*. *Animations* are applied to *objects* or *elements* on a slide.

Exactly What *Is* a Transition Effect?

A transition effect is a method of changing from one slide to another. This may be a subtle **Fade** effect or something dramatic like the **Curtains** transition, which simulates curtains being opened when a slide is presented. If applied correctly, transitions can boost visual appeal by introducing an element of motion.

If you start with a blank presentation, each slide displays with no transition effects. If you use a template, there may or may not be a transition effect already applied to one or more slides.

How Do You Apply a Transition to a Slide?

Starting in PowerPoint 2010, there are separate tabs for **Transitions** and **Animations**. To apply a transition to a slide, follow these steps:

1. In **Normal** view, click on the slide thumbnail on the left to select a slide.
2. From the **Transitions** tab, click on a transition.
3. A preview of the transition is shown. To see the applied transition again, click **Preview** on the far left.
4. To select a different transition, just select another transition from the **Ribbon**. Since you can only have one transition per slide, only the last transition you select is applied to the current slide.

Quick Tip – How Do You Apply the Same Transition to Multiple Slides?

To apply the same transition to multiple slides, press the CTRL key while clicking on slide thumbnails to select non-adjacent slides, or press the SHIFT key while clicking to select a range of adjacent slides; then apply the transition.

Transitions have been enhanced in later versions of PowerPoint. The images below compare **Transitions** in PowerPoint 2007 and PowerPoint 2016.

As you can see, newer versions of PowerPoint, such as PowerPoint 2016, offer more transitions and provides a description of each type of transition.

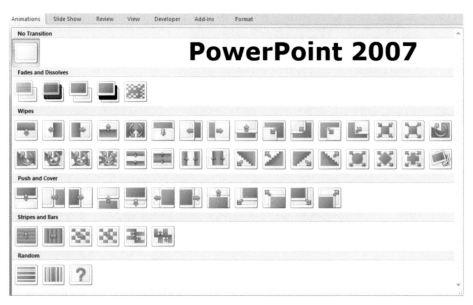

Quick Tip – My Favorite Slide Transition Picks

- *My favorite **Slide Transition** for a subtle, professional approach is **Fade**.*
- *My favorite **Slide Transition** for a cool approach is either **Push** or **Wipe**.*
- *My favorite **Slide Transition** for an ultra-cool approach is **Drape**.*
- *My favorite **Slide Transition** for a dramatic opening is **Vortex**.*

*Note: **Transitions** may vary in different versions of PowerPoint.*

View Companion Video #16 to see these steps in action

Go to www.youtube.com and search for **#ezppt16**

#17: Animation Example 1: Creating a Color-Changing Sound Wave Image

Scenario: You are an Instructional Designer and have been asked to animate a sound wave image so that it changes into different colors as music plays. *How do you accomplish this?*

Let's get started.

1. On a new slide, insert your image via **Insert**-> **Pictures**. In this example, a free sound wave image from pixabay.com is being used (see image below). You will need multiple versions of your image in different colors. In this example, we'll explore the available **Recolor** options within PowerPoint. These steps can be applied to any type of image where you want to simulate a color-changing effect; however, depending on the type of image, you may need to use an external photo editor to edit image colors beforehand.
2. Double-click on your image to open the **Format** tab.
3. Click **Color** to open the drop-down menu.
4. In the **Recolor** section, hover over the color options, and click to select your first color choice.
5. Next, let's apply an **Entrance Fade** effect to your image. With the image selected, click the **Animations** tab; then click **Fade**. In the **Timing** group, change **Start** to **After Previous**, and set the **Duration** to 1.25 (1.25 seconds) for now. You can edit the duration of one or more images later to synchronize to music if needed. Now you have prepared your first image with fade effect and timing.
6. Next, duplicate the image several times. With your image selected, press **CTRL + D** to duplicate in one step! Duplicate your image 4 times.
7. For each duplicate image, repeat steps 2 through 4 above to apply a different color to each image. At this point, you should have five images in different colors, with the **Fade** effect and timing already applied.

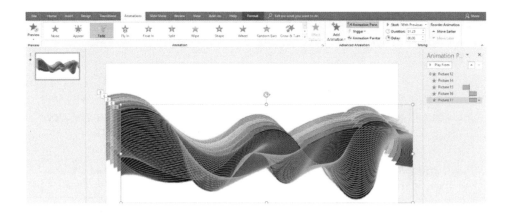

8. Now you'll ready to put it all together. To create the color-changing simulation, stack the images on top of each in the exact same position. Here's how:
    a. Select all your images by pressing **CTRL + A**.
    b. From the **Home** tab, in the **Drawing** group, click **Arrange-> Align-> Align Center**; then click **Arrange-> Align-> Align Middle**.
9. Your color-changing simulation animation is ready! Click **Slide Show-> From Beginning**.
10. To lengthen the animation:
    a. Select all your images by pressing **CTRL + A**.
    b. Then copy all your images (**CTRL + C**).
    c. Click outside the slide to unselect your images.
    d. Then click Paste (**CTRL + V**) to paste a second set of images. To align the second set of images, repeat step 8b above. Now you have double the images for a lengthier color-changing simulation animation.
11. Finally, let's add some music. Click **Insert-> Audio-> Audio on My PC**. Then select the music of your choice. To setup the audio to play in the background automatically, from the **Playback** tab, click **Play in Background**. You may also want to hide the audio object that displays by right clicking on the object and selecting **Send to Back**.
12. Press F5 to instantly start your slideshow and see the animation in action!

To see a full demonstration of all steps above, be sure to use the link below for the companion video.

View Companion Video #17 to see these steps in action

Go to www.youtube.com and search for *#ezppt17*

#18: Animation Example 2: Spinning Game Wheel with Simulated Lights

Scenario: You work in the IT department for a casino, and you've been asked to create an animation for a casino game advertisement. All that was provided to you was a flat image of a game wheel.

Requirements:

- Create a simulation around the wheel which looks like lights flashing.
- After the flashing lights stop, the game wheel needs to spin automatically for four seconds.

How do you accomplish this? To simulate lights flashing, layers of circular shapes can be placed around the wheel in different colors; by setting up layers of different colored circles to display consecutively but with a slight delay, it will appear as if the lights are flashing. To get the wheel to spin, apply the **Spin** effect which is available in the **Emphasis** section of **Animations** options. To have it spin for four seconds, you can set the **Duration** to 4:00 seconds.

Here's a summary of how to setup the animation:

1. On a new slide, insert your image via **Insert**-> **Pictures**. In this example, a free game wheel image from pixabay.com is being used. If needed, use **Remove Background** to remove the background from your image. In the **Animations** tab, select the **Spin** effect located in the **Emphasis** animations. Finally, change **Start** to **After Previous** and set the **Duration** to four seconds in the **Timing** group. Click **Preview** on the left of the Animations tab to see how it looks so far.
2. To create an illusion of lights blinking, do the following:
   a. On a second blank slide, draw a circle larger than the game wheel (remember to hold down the **SHIFT** key while you draw the circle to make it symmetrical). Select red (or another dark bright color) for the fill color.
   b. Next, draw a small white symmetrical circle on the edge of the red circle (see image below to get an idea of the size); duplicate it 27 times (the number of white circles needed may vary depending on the size of your circles). **Quick Tip:** With the first

small white circle selected, press **CTRL + D** repeatedly (27 times or as many times as needed to duplicate your white circles). This saves you from having to use copy/paste.

    c.   Position all the small white circles around the inner edge of the large red circle, as shown in the image below. To help with alignment, from the **View,** check the **Gridlines** checkbox).

3.   Next, you will need another version of the red circle with smaller circles for another layer. For now, duplicate the slide by doing the following: click the slide thumbnail to select it; then press **CTRL + D** to duplicate the slide. You should now have three slides, one with the game wheel, and two more slides with the same image (large red circle with small white circles).

4.   On the third slide, change the color of every other small white circle to yellow. This can be done easily through the use of the **Format Painter**.

    a.   First, select one small white circle; change the fill color to yellow.

    b.   Next, click on the yellow circle to select it, then double-click **Format Painter** in the **Ribbon**. Your mouse pointer should have a small paint brush image displayed.

    c.   Single click on every other white circle to apply (paint) the yellow color fill accordingly. Your three slides should now look like this:

5. Next, it's important to group all your circular shapes together on each slide so they will stay put, and to make the images easy to move or copy. First, click on slide 2; select all shapes (**CTRL + A**); right click and select **Group**. (be sure to point to an edge of the selected images when you select **Group**; otherwise, you will lose your selection). Repeat these steps for slide 3.

6. Now the grouped shapes (one image) from slide 3 need to be layered on top of the image on slide 2. Click on the image on slide 3 (that's the red circle with the small white and yellow circles); click **Cut (CTRL + X)**; go to slide 2 and click **Paste (CTRL + V)**.

7. Now both red circular images are on slide 2. Click **CTRL + A** to select both images. Before we apply animation effects, let's duplicate the images several times. With the images selected, click **CTRL + D** to duplicate. Repeat this about 8 or 10 times.

8. Next, to arrange all images so that they are in the exact same position, first click **CTRL + A** to select all images. Next, from the **Home** tab, click **Arrange-> Align-> Align Center**; then click **Arrange-> Align-> Align Middle**. All images should now be stacked on top of each other in the same position (it will give the illusion that there is only one image).

9. Next, apply the animation. With all images selected, from the **Animations** tab, click **Appear**. In the **Timing** group, change **Start** to **After Previous**, and change the **Duration** to .5 (1/2 second).

10. Now might be a good time to see how the animation looks on slide 2. Click **Preview** on the left of the Animation tab. You should see the layers appearing one by one, first a red circle with all small white circles, then a red circle with small white and yellow circles. It will give the illusion of blinking lights.

11. Finally, let's add the game wheel image to the center of the images on slide 2. Go to slide 1, select the game wheel image and select **Cut** (CTRL + X); go to slide 2 and select **Paste (CTRL + V)**. Now you'll need to resize the game wheel so that it fits correctly in the center of the red circular image. Make sure the game wheel image is selected. While holding the **SHIFT** key down, point to one of the corner handles, and drag inward to resize. To reposition the wheel, move the mouse until you see a four-headed arrow, then drag the image to reposition as needed.

12. Your slide 2 should now look something like the image below. Click **Preview** on the left to see the animation.

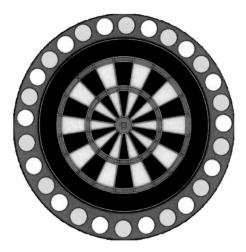

That's it! Your spinning game wheel with simulated flashing lights is finished.

Reminders:

- Remember to delete the extra slides (slides 1 and 3).
- Save often when creating this animation and make backup copies of your work.
- Some timing adjustments may be needed in order for the spinning wheel with the blinking lights animations to work together.
- Remember the **Spin** Animation is not an **Entrance** animation, so the wheel will display first, then the **Spinning** will begin thereafter. You can experiment with the Start options in the **Timing** group to determine whether **After Previous** or **With Previous** works best for you.
- To see a full demonstration of all steps above, be sure to use the link below for the companion video.

View Companion Video #18 to see these steps in action

Go to www.youtube.com and search for ***#ezppt18***

#19:   Animation Example 3: Text Animations

Scenario: You are a Sales Representative, and you are giving a presentation on a new marketing strategy tomorrow morning. You have already created your presentation, but it has no animation or special effects as of yet. Your slides contain more text than images. You have been asked by your manager to add some animation to your text. How can this be accomplished quickly and easily?

You may have seen presentations where text seems to magically appear on the screen like a ghost is printing the text. There are several ways to do this. **Note**: If you're looking for a simulation of a hand image writing text, this is covered in section #21. Let's look at a few different options for text animations.

1. On a blank slide, type the text: **Marketing Strategy Session.**
2. Select the text. **Quick Tip**: Triple-click to select all text. You can also press **CTRL + A**.
3. In the **Font** drop-down menu, select **Segoe Print** or **Segoe Script**. **Note**: You can use any font, but these particular fonts or something similar works well with the animations we are about to apply since they resemble handwriting.

Option #1: Wipe From Left

a. From the **Animations** tab, select **Wipe** from the **Entrance** animations.
b. By default, the **Wipe** animation is set to **From Bottom**. Let's change that to a different direction. From the **Animations** tab, click the drop-down arrow for **Effect Options** and select **From Left**.
c. Click **Preview** on the left of the **Animations** tab to see what it looks like so far. As you can see, it's quite fast and doesn't really look like a printing simulation just yet. Let's slow it down. To view more options for the **Wipe** animation, click the small diagonal arrow at the bottom of **Effect Options**.
d. The **Wipe** dialog box displays. Click the drop-down arrow to view **Animate Text** options. Select **By letter**; for the **% delay between letters**, change 10 to 60.
e. Click **Preview** on the left of the **Animations** tab to see the effect.

Option #2: Fade

a. From the **Animations** tab, select **Fade** from the **Entrance** animations.
b. To view more options for the **Fade** animation, click the small diagonal arrow at the bottom of **Effect Options**.
c. The **Fade** dialog box displays. Click the drop-down arrow to view **Animate Text** options. Select **By letter**; for the **% delay between letters**, change 10 to 40.
d. Click **Preview** on the left of the **Animations** tab to see the effect.

Option #3: Peek In From Left

a. Before applying this next effect, clear any animations already applied. To remove animations, just click the animation number (which displays when the **Animation** tab is selected) and press **Delete**. For this next effect, from the **Animations** tab, click **Add Animation-> More Entrance Effects;** then from the **Basic** section, select **Peek in**, then click **OK.**
b. By default, the **Peek In** animation is set to **From Bottom**. Let's change that to a different direction. From the **Animations** tab, click the drop-down arrow for **Effect Options** and select **From Left**.
c. To view more options for the **Peek In** animation, click the small diagonal arrow at the bottom of **Effect Options**.
d. The **Peek In** dialog box displays. Click the drop-down arrow to view **Animate Text** options. Select **By letter**; for the **% delay between letters**, change 10 to 40.
e. Click **Preview** on the left of the **Animations** tab to see the effect.

Option #4: Dissolve In

a. Before applying this next effect, clear any animations already applied. To remove animations, just click the animation number (which displays when the Animation tab is selected) and press **Delete**. For this next effect, from the **Animations** tab, click **Add Animation-> More Entrance Effects;** then from the **Basic** section, select **Dissolve In**, then click **OK.**

b. To view more options for the **Dissolve In** animation, click the small diagonal arrow at the bottom of **Effect Options**.

c. The **Dissolve In** dialog box displays. Click the drop-down arrow to view **Animate Text** options. Select **By letter**; for the **% delay between letters**, change 10 to 40.

d. Click **Preview** on the left of the **Animations** tab to see the effect.

For all the options above, you can experiment with the **% delay between letters** in the animation **Effect Options** as needed to increase or decrease the speed.

View Companion Video #19 to see these steps in action

Go to www.youtube.com and search for *#ezppt19*

#20: Using Motion Paths Part 1: Skiing Down a Mountain Simulation

Another type of animation is **Motion Paths**, which includes **Lines, Arcs, Turns, Shapes, Loops,** and **Custom Paths**. Choosing **Custom Paths** allows you draw your own path for the object you are animating; where the other options have pre-formatted paths or directions for your animation. There are additional **Motion Path** options by selecting "**More Motions Paths...**"

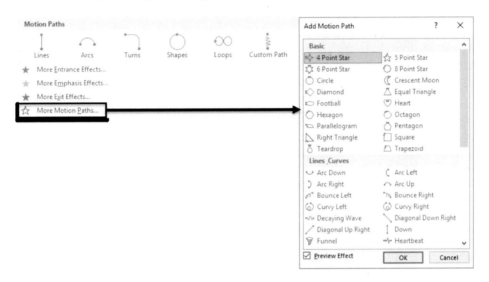

What Can Motion Paths Be Used For?

- **Fun Stuff:**
    o Show a car driving down a path
    o Simulate a plane flying across the sky
    o Animate someone skiing down a mountain (see example below)
    o Animate someone drawing or show a picture being drawn
- **Education and Demonstrations:**
    o Simulate a flower growing and teach about gardening
    o Simulate a rock falling down a mountain and teach about falling rocks and avalanches
    o Simulate fish swimming in water and teach about the ocean
- **Business Presentations:**
    o Demonstrate a process flow with an animated line or other shape

- o Demonstrate the journey of a project from start to finish
- o Simulate someone writing in cursive to emphasize words in a presentation (see example in the next section #21)

The possibilities are endless. Remember, animations can be used for a variety of things, in different industries, for education, business, training, demonstrations, presentations, or just plain fun.

In this example, we will demonstrate how to show someone skiing down a mountain. We'll start with a winter scene for the background. Next an image of a skier with a transparent background is added to the scene. The image of the skier is positioned at the top of the mountain and rotated slightly so it is aligned with the top of the mountain. Note: To rotate an image, with the image selected, point to the curved arrow at the top of the image using your mouse, then move left or right to rotate.

To draw a motion path for the skier image:

1. Click the image of the skier to select the image.
2. Click the **Animations** tab (if it's not already open) to view animation options.
3. Click **More** (that's the drop-down arrow with the horizontal line to the right of the animations) to view all animation options.

4. Select **Custom Paths**.
5. Your mouse pointer changes into a cross hair symbol. Position your mouse at the starting point; then press and drag your mouse to draw your custom path. Release your mouse, then press the Escape key (ESC) on your keyboard to end the path.
6. The animation immediately plays. If the path is not how you would like it to be, press CTRL + Z to undo and repeat steps 2 to 5 above and try again.

View Companion Video #20 to see these steps in action

Go to www.youtube.com and search for ***#ezppt20***

#21: Using Motion Paths Part 2: Handwriting/Drawing Animation

You may have seen videos of a person's hand drawing a picture, or simulated handwriting animations during a presentation? There are lots of tools used to create these animations, but did you know you can create similar animations and simulations using special effects and motion paths?

Handwriting Text Animation

To draw a motion path to simulate someone writing or printing text:

1. On a blank slide, type the text: **Have a Nice Day.**
2. Select the text. **Quick Tip**: Triple-click to select all text. You can also press **CTRL + A**.
3. In the **Font** drop-down menu, select a font. If you want the animation to look like handwriting, there are a number of fonts available that resemble handwriting, including **Brush Script Std, Segoe Print** or **Segoe Script**.
4. Next, obtain an image of a hand holding a pen or pencil, and insert the image on your slide. For now, move it away from the text.
5. First, let's add animation to the text.
   a. Select your text (triple-click or press **CTRL + A**).
   b. Click the **Animations** tab.
   c. Click **Appear**.
   d. Next, click the small diagonal arrow at the bottom of **Effect Options**.
   e. The **Appear** dialog box displays. Click the drop-down arrow to view **Animate Text** options. Select **By letter.** For the **% delay between letters**, change .5 to .425 (you will understand why in a later step). Click **OK**.
   f. Click Preview on the left of the **Animations** tab to see the effect.
6. Next, let's add animation to the hand image.
   a. Click to select the hand image.
   b. In the **Animations** tab, click **More** (that's the drop-down arrow with the horizontal line to the right of the animations) to view all animation options.

c. Select **Custom Paths**.

d. Your mouse pointer changes into a cross hair symbol. Position your mouse at the starting point of the text; then press and drag your mouse to draw your custom path, carefully drawing the path as if you were writing the text. Be sure to keep your left mouse button pressed the whole time while you are drawing the path. When you are finished drawing the path, release your mouse, then press the **Escape** key (**ESC**) on your keyboard to end the path.

7. The animation immediately plays. If the path is not how you would like it to be, press **CTRL + Z** to undo and repeat steps a through d above and try again.

8. Once the custom path animation is completed, in order to synchronize it with the text animation, first, in the **Timing** group, change **Start** to **With Previous**.

9. Next, do the following to correctly position the hand at the starting point of the first character.

a. Click **Preview** to test the animation.

b. Adjust the position of the hand so that the pencil or pen point is at the beginning of the first character of the text when the animation plays. This may take a few tries. Repeat steps a and b as needed.

10. Finally, some timing changes are needed so that the hand animation and text animation play at the same time from start to finish. To check the current timing for the hand animation, with the hand image selected, click the small diagonal arrow at the bottom of **Effect Options**. Click the **Timing** tab; then click the drop-down for the **Duration** field. Select **5 seconds (Very Slow)**. **Note**: You may need to adjust the **Duration** depending on the desired speed of your animation.

11. To calculate the amount of time it will take for the text animation to play, multiply the total number of characters in the text by the **% delay between letters** (which was set to .425 in step 5e. above). There are 12 characters in the text, so 12 multiplied by .425 equals 5.1 seconds. This is pretty close to 5 seconds. **Note**: You may need to adjust the **% delay between letters** to synchronize it just right.

12. Click **Preview** on the left of the **Animations** tab to see the effect. Your animation is now completed!

The image below is an example of how the text and custom path looks on the slide.

Remember to follow the link at the end of this section to see a full demonstration of all steps above.

Drawing a Picture Animation

To simulate someone drawing a picture, you don't actually need to draw the exact path of the drawing process. Using a black and white drawing, you can use an **Entrance** animation to slowly display the drawing, then create a custom path and just scribble left and right or up and down to simulate drawing.

For example, in the image below, a circular drawing of stick figures is added to the slide; then the **Wheel Entrance** animation is added to the image. This will allow the circular image to appear slowly in a clockwise direction. If the shape of your drawing is square, consider using **Appear**, **Fade** or **Wipe** animation. **Note**: If you are using the Wipe animation, change the direction to **From Left**.

Next, an image of a hand is added, then a custom path using an up and down scribble motion is added. You can use the same steps in the previous handwriting example to add the custom path.

The image below shows both images including the custom path drawn to simulate the drawing of the circular black and white drawing.

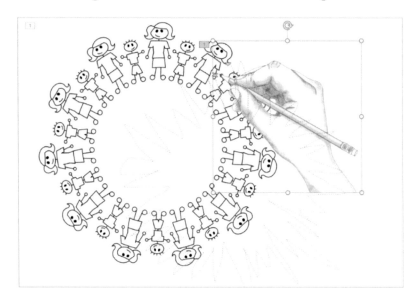

View Companion Video #21 to see these steps in action

Go to www.youtube.com and search for *#ezppt21*

Part VII: *Extras*

Contents

Extras

Speaker Notes and Audience Handouts (Including PDF Conversion)

Adding and Formatting Hyperlinks

Converting a PowerPoint to a Video (MP4)

More Tips and Secret Tricks!

#22: Speaker Notes and Audience Handouts (Including PDF Conversion)

Scenario: You are speaking at a large convention, and you will be delivering your presentation in person to approximately 100 guests. In addition, there are 75 people who will be viewing your presentation live via WebEx. You have memorized your speaker notes, but for reference, you need a printout of the text content contained on your slides, as well as your slide notes.

In addition, you have been asked to provide two types of handouts for visitors:

- First, you need a paper handout with slide thumbnails (3 per page) so they can follow along during the presentation and take notes along the way.
- Second, you need to convert your presentation to a PDF web-friendly format for your online attendees.

How to Print Speaker Notes and Slide Show Outline

To print your slides with slide notes, do the following:

1. Click **File-> Print**.
2. In the **Settings** area, by default, **Full Page Slides** is selected. Click the drop-down arrow in the **Full Page Slides** field and select **Notes Pages**. This will generate a printout of all your slides, with one slide per page including any notes which were entered in the **Notes** area for each slide.
3. Click **Print**.

How to Print a Slide Show Outline

To print an outline of your presentation, including all text content from your slides, you can select to print an outline by doing the following:

1. Click **File-> Print**.

2. In the **Settings** area, by default, **Full Page Slides** is selected. Click the drop-down arrow in the **Full Page Slides** field and select **Outline**.
3. Click **Print**.

How to Print Handouts with Slide Thumbnails

To print audience handouts of your slides, with 3 slide thumbnails per page, do the following:

1. Click **File**-> **Print**.
2. In the **Settings** area, by default, **Full Page Slides** is selected. Click the drop-down arrow in the **Full Page Slides** field; under **Handouts**, select 3 Page. To change the orientation from landscape to portrait, in the **Orientation** drop-down, select **Portrait**.
3. Click **Print**.

Note: In earlier versions of PowerPoint, a **Print** dialog displays instead of the print pane on the left. Starting in PowerPoint 2013, a Print options pane displays on the left, although the print options are primarily the same. The images below show the differences in how 3-slide handouts are printed in older (2007) vs. newer (2016) versions of PowerPoint.

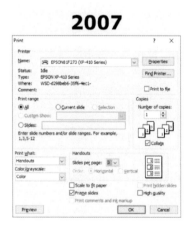

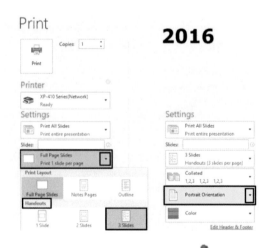

Need to save ink? Before printing, click the drop-down for **Printer** and select **Microsoft Print to PDF**. After making this selection, a dialog box displays prompting you to enter a destination location to save your PDF. For more PDF save options, see the steps below on how to convert our slide show to PDF format.

Converting a Slide Show to a PDF Document

To convert your slide show to PDF file format, do the following:

1. Click **File-> Save As**.
2. Select a **Save As** option to specify the destination location to save your file. In this example, select **Browse**. This option displays the old familiar **Save As** dialog box.
3. Navigate to the desired drive and location.
4. Enter a file name for your file in the File name field (don't include a file extension).
5. In the **Save as Type** field, click the drop-down arrow to view available file formats.
6. Select **PDF (*.pdf)**.
7. Notice there are some additional options at the bottom of the **Save As** dialog box. Click the **Options** button. From the **Options** dialog box, you can change the slide range, specify what to include (Slides, Handouts, Notes Page, Outline View) and even specify if your PDF document is PDF/A compliant. This compliance feature is an important option to have checked if you are converting a book to be published.
8. Click **OK**.
9. Click **Save**.
10. Your PDF document will open momentarily.

Your PowerPoint slide show has now been converted to a PDF. Please note that the PDF version of your slide show will not contain any animations or transitions. If your slide show contains animations or other media, such as video or audio, see section #24 on how to convert a PowerPoint file to video format.

View Companion Video #22 to see these steps in action

Go to www.youtube.com and search for ***#ezppt22***

#23: *Adding and Formatting Hyperlinks*

Using Hyperlinks for Navigation

Did you also know that you can create links to other slides in your presentation and create custom navigation buttons as well? This can be used for a table of contents and for linking to specific slides.

Creating Links for a Table of Contents

Let's say you have a series of training modules and each module is a series of pages in your PowerPoint document. You can easily create a table of contents for your presentation and create links from the topics in the table of contents to link to other pages.

Your table of contents can either be text or objects such as buttons. Let's say you have five lessons as part of your training program, as shown below.

Training Outline

Lesson 1: Introduction to Marketing
Lesson 2: Marketing Planning and Strategies
Lesson 3: Customer Relationship Marketing
Lesson 4: Product Development
Lesson 5: Case Studies

First, create all the pages for your presentation. Then return to the table of contents and do the following to create links for each of the lessons in your presentation:

1. Select the text. For example, select "Lesson 1: Introduction to Marketing."
2. Click **Insert-> Link**, or right-click and select **Hyperlink**.
3. On the left, select **Place in This Document**.

4. A list of all slides displays in the **Select a place in this document** section. Click to select the page to link to.
5. Click **OK**.

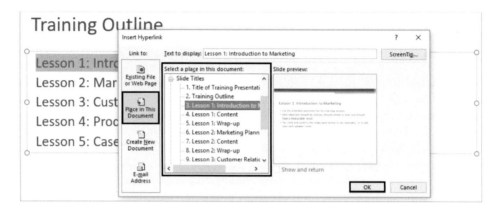

Repeat the steps for each word, topic, or phrase you need to link to in your table of contents.

You can easily change the text into more visually appealing buttons. Just right-click on each text box and add a fill color and outline color if desired.

You can also insert shapes as well. Once you insert a shape, just start typing text. Additional shape formatting options are also available. Just right-click on the edge of a shape and select **Format Shape**.

Navigation Buttons

You can also add navigation buttons in the same manner using text boxes or shapes. You can also consider inserting images as buttons. However, if images are inserted, you will need to overlay text boxes on the images, and then link the image, text box, or both to another slide. As an alternative, you can use a photo editor outside of PowerPoint to format a button image with text, then insert and link the image to the corresponding slide.

Examples of navigational buttons: Home, Previous, and Next.

Once you have your text boxes or shape images created, just click **Insert-> Link** and select the corresponding slide to link to. Here's an example of what your slides might look like with navigational buttons:

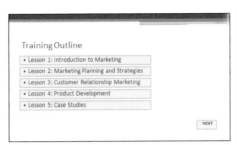 

Quick Tip – Disabling PageUp/PageDown and Scrolling During a Slide Show

*If you create navigational buttons in your slide show, you may not want your learners or audience to have the ability to scroll or use the PageUp and PageDown keys. To disable PageUp and PageDown as well as scrolling, click **Slide Show**, **Setup Slide Show**, and select the radio button, **Browsed at a kiosk (full screen)**.*

Hyperlinking to External Websites

Linking to external websites is just as easy. To create a link to a specific URL, do the following:

1. Select the text, image or other object to be linked.
2. Click **Insert-> Link**, or right-click and select **Hyperlink**.

3. On the left, select to link to **Existing File or Web Page**.
4. Type the website address in the **Address** field.
5. Click **OK**.

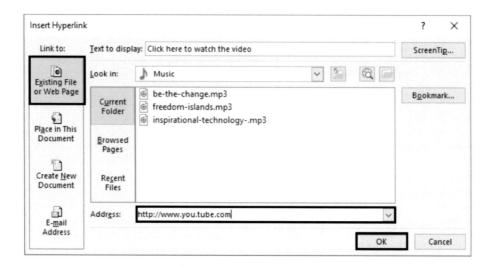

 Quick Tip – Creating Hyperlinks in a Snap

*If you type an actual website address (URL) such as www.google.com on a slide (with a www prefix), when you press ENTER, a hyperlink is automatically added on your slide. To change the text that displays on your slide, right click on the link, select **Edit Link**, and type your custom text in the **Text to display** box at the top of the **Insert Hyperlink** dialog box.*

Creating an Interactive PDF (iPDF)

When you create hyperlinks in PowerPoint, all the links are preserved when you save your PowerPoint file to PDF file format. In section #22 you learned how to use **File-> Save As** to save to .pdf file format. You can use the same steps to save your PowerPoint file containing hyperlinks to a PDF file.

After saving your file to .pdf file format, be sure to test all the hyperlinks thoroughly. Although all hyperlinks are preserved, testing is essential to ensure all links are working properly.

Even though PDF file format is web-friendly on a computer or laptop, it may not be mobile ready. Be sure to test your iPDF on mobile devices, including iPhones, Android devices, iPads and tablets. If your iPDF is not displaying properly on your mobile device, you may need to optimize your PDF to make it mobile-ready using third-party software such as Adobe Acrobat Pro, which has a specific conversion tool to optimize PDF files for mobile devices.

View Companion Video #23 to see these steps in action

Go to www.youtube.com and search for **#ezppt23**

#24: *Converting a PowerPoint to a Video (MP4)*

Scenario: You have created a self-running slide show packed with animations, voice over, and music. You have been asked to convert your slide show into a web-friendly format to be uploaded to your company's website for employees to view remotely. You can't convert your presentation to PDF because the animations and sound will not work in a PDF document. How do you convert your presentation to video format?

Beginning in PowerPoint 2013, you can convert your PowerPoint file directly to MP4 (.mp4) format. MP4 (.mp4) is the digital format multimedia format most commonly used to store video and allows streaming over the Internet. If you are creating a video for YouTube, MP4 (.mp4) is the preferred video format for optimum quality.

To convert your slide show to MP4 (.mp4) format, do the following:

1. Select **File-> Save As**.
2. Click the location where you would like to save your video.
3. In the **Save As Type** field, select **MPEG-4 Video (*.mp4)**.
4. Click **Save**.
5. At the bottom of the screen, a progress bar will display during the conversion. This will take several minutes depending on the size of your file. If you need to cancel the conversion, click the X in the circle to the right of the progress bar.
6. After the conversion, to view your video, minimize your PowerPoint window and navigate to the location where the file was saved using File Explorer (in Windows 10), or Windows Explorer (prior to Windows 10). **Note**: Windows Explorer, not to be confused with Internet Explorer, was renamed to File Explorer starting with Windows 10.

Note: Unfortunately, the option to save to MP4 (.mp4) file format is not available for versions earlier than PowerPoint 2013. As an alternative, you can save to Windows Media Video (.wmv), but this format requires a software program such as Windows Media Player, RealPlayer, MPlayer, or VLC Media Player in order the play the video. You can also use other software programs to convert Windows Media Video (.wmv) to MP4 (.mp4) file format.

View Companion Video #24 to see these steps in action

Go to www.youtube.com and search for *#ezppt24*

#25:   *More Tips and Secret Tricks!*

Hiding Your Screen During a Presentation

Did you ever wish you could temporarily hide your presentation? You can! While in slide show mode, press the letter B on your keyboard to change the screen to black while presenting. Press the B again on your keyboard to bring your presentation back. Just remember, B for black and B brings it back!

Does Anyone Have a Pen?

While in slide show mode, if you need to annotate, just press **CTRL+P** for the **Pen** tool. Then use your mouse to draw or write directly on your slide. You can still navigate through your slide show as usual with the Pen tool on. When you move to a new slide, you can draw or write on the next slide if needed; or, to turn off the Pen, just press **CTRL+P** again.

Removing the Background of an Image

If you layer one image on top of another, some images may not have a transparent background. If your image has a white background and you need it to be transparent, there's a little trick you can do in PowerPoint to remove the background. First, click on the image, then click **Remove Background** from the **Adjust** group in the ribbon. PowerPoint will make an educated guess as to what area of the image you would like to remove. Use the handles to adjust and then experiment to remove the background of your image. Click **Mark Areas to Keep**, or **Mark Areas to Discard** as needed. When finished, click **Keep Changes** or **Discard All Changes**.

Awesome Templates That Will Blow Your Socks Off!!

The newer versions of PowerPoint offer newer, cooler, more innovative templates than ever! Here are 3 that you don't want to miss. Click **File-> New**; then search for the following templates:

Powerful Presentations – Available in PowerPoint 2013 and 2016, this template was created by Neal Creative and contains cool special effects and contains a rich assortment of animated slides.

3D PowerPoint Presentation – Available in PowerPoint 2016, this template shows a Hubble Space Telescope Model with sample 3D views. It also explains how Office 365 subscribers can add 3D models to documents and rotate the angle to show the right view.

Statistics Infographics Sampler – Available in PowerPoint 2016, this template contains a variety of cool infographics, which are customizable. Also included is a sample of the PowerPoint Graphics library available on getmygraphics.com which is owned by eLearning Brothers.

Grouping and Ungroup Objects in Templates

Did you know that for certain templates, you can ungroup some of the more complex graphics to customize them for your presentations? For example, the **Statistics Infographics Sampler** template found in PowerPoint 2016 contains a variety of slides with complex graphics that you can ungroup. To **Ungroup**, right-click on an image and select **Ungroup,** if available. Here is an example of one of the slides containing a complex graphic which can be ungrouped (the grouped images on the left are ungrouped):

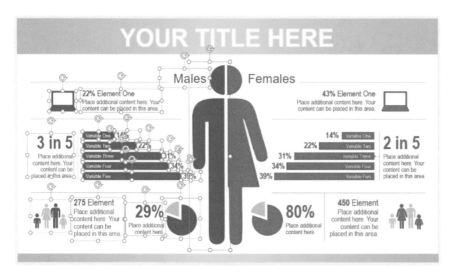

Extra Features Available With the Office 365 Subscription Service

If you are considering upgrading to a new version of Office, as an alternative to purchasing an upgrade or a full version, or if you don't currently have Microsoft Office, Microsoft also has a subscription service called Office 365. The advantage to the subscription service is that it provides the latest version of Office software including PowerPoint. In addition, Office 365 has some bonus features. One cool bonus feature is called the **Morph** transition. This feature allows you to create a morphing animation using two slides with similar images, creating a smooth animation between two objects. If you own Office 365, here's how to use the morph effect: right-click on the slide thumbnail containing an object and click **Duplicate** (or press **CTRL + D**). On the duplicate slide, make a change to the object size, shape or color. From the **Transitions** tab, click **Morph**. Click **Preview** in the Ribbon or play your slide show and see the result.

Function Key Shortcuts

F1   Need Help? Press F1 anytime to display the **Help** pane to search for Help on a specific topic. For additional guidance, you can enter a word or phrase in the "Tell me what you want to do" box on the right of the menu above the ribbon.

F5   To instantly start your slide show, press F5.

F12   You may already be using **CTRL + S** to quickly save your presentation. But what if you want to make a copy of your presentation using a new filename? You can either click **File**, **Save As**, or just press **F12** to instantly display the **Save As** dialog box.

Keyboard Shortcuts

CTRL + A = Select All
within a text box.

Select all objects on a slide or select all text

CTRL + B = Bold

Apply bold to the selected text.

CTRL + C = Copy
clipboard.

Copy selected object(s) or slide(s) to the

CTRL + D = Duplicate
thumbnail.

Quickly duplicate the selected object or slide

CTRL + F = Search

Search for a word or phrase.

CTRL + H = Replace

Find and Replace text.

CTRL + I = Italics

Apply italics to the selected text.

CTRL + K = Hyperlink

Insert a Hyperlink.

CTRL + M = New Slide

Insert a new slide in the current location.

CTRL + N = New File

Start a new blank presentation.

CTRL + O = Open
presentation.

Same as File-> Open; open an existing

CTRL + P = Print

Same as File-> Print; open the print options.

CTRL + Q = Close
presentation.

Same as File-> Close; close the current

CTRL + T = Font
box).

Opens the Font dialog box (from inside a text

CTRL + V = Paste
clipboard.

Paste the object(s) or slide(s) from the

CTRL + Z = Undo

Undo the last command.

More Keyboard Shortcuts From Within a Text Box:

- To go to the beginning of a line, press the **Home** key.
- To go to the end of a line, press **the** End key.
- To quickly navigate to the very top of the text box, press CTRL + HOME.
- To move to the end of the text box, press CTRL + END.

Mouse Shortcuts

Double Click   Select a word (from within a text box)

Triple Click   Select All (same as **CTRL + A**)

CTRL + Click   Select non-adjacent slide thumbnails

SHIFT + Click   Select a range of slide thumbnails or select multiple objects on a slide

CTRL + TAB   Switch between PowerPoint windows.

View Companion Video #25 to see these steps in action

Go to www.youtube.com and search for *#ezppt25*

keyboardshortcuts

CTRL + end = last slide

CTRL + Home = first slide

Many Thanks!

I hope you have enjoyed learning these tips, tricks, shortcuts, and a few little "secrets" in Microsoft PowerPoint.

Thank you for purchasing this book!

Visit Easylearningweb's YouTube channel
http://www.youtube.com/user/easylearningweb for online training videos.

Want more tips, tricks and shortcuts?

Visit http://www.easylearningweb.com for the latest updates on new books, articles, videos and more!

Can I ask for a small favor? Could you please take a minute or two and leave a review on Amazon? Please visit http://www.amazon.com/feedback.

Your review will help me improve content in future books.

Thank you in advance for your feedback!

Amelia

Other Books in the Series by Amelia Griggs:

Other 7 X 10 Color Versions:

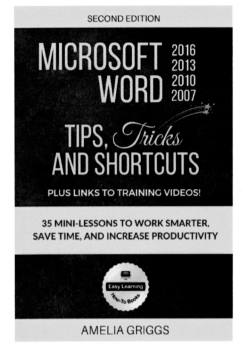 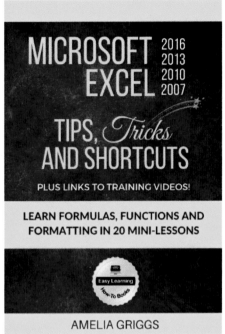

Large Print 8 X 10 Black and White Version for PowerPoint book is also available.

Other Black and White Versions are also available. Be sure to click to view all formats for all listings on: http://www.amazon.com/author/ameliagriggs

To be notified when new books and videos are available, get links to new blog articles and be alerted for book giveaways and free gifts, join the Easy Learning Newsletter, visit:
http://www.easylearningweb.com

http://eepurl.com/cNULVr

Don't miss out! Join Today!

52166101R00082

Made in the USA
Middletown, DE
08 July 2019